The COMMUNICATIONS Handbook

$ 6.20

NELSON CANADA

ACKNOWLEDGMENTS

Senior Editor:
- Paula S. Goepfert

The Communications Handbook is based on a project initiated by the Strathcona County Board of Education, Alberta.

Originating Senior Editor:
- Patriciamay F. McBlane

Originating Assistant Editors:
- Robert P. Johnston
- Rorri McBlane

The Publisher gratefully acknowledges the contributions of:
- William W. Sime, Assistant Superintendent of Curriculum and Instruction
- Shirley White
- The students and teachers of the Board, specifically:

F. Belyea	E. Matwichuk
T. Burron	T. Miller
M. Ceretzke	J. Naslund
A. Dixon	D. Nelson
B. Drysdale	J. Nelson
D. Fjested	C. Plattor
D. Footz	H. Sadee
I. Foster	H. Saranchuk
M. Franke	V. Schulmeister
D. Griffiths	T. Stapleton
O. Grundholm	D. Stewart
L. Harris	J. Taylor
E. Hefford	G. Topolniski
R. Henning	S. Topolniski
T. Keelor	L. Williams
H. Kerley	M. Williston
E. Lindman	L. Zucker
A. Long	

- Grace McPike, Language Arts Consultant

Contributing Editors:
- Mary Robson
- Jonathan Kaplan
- Peggy Foy

Design and Cover:
- Paul Kaufhold

Published in 1982 by
Nelson Canada
A Division of International
Thomson Limited, 1982
1120 Birchmount Road
Scarborough, Ontario

Printed and bound in Canada
ISBN 0-17-601507-8

Canadian Cataloguing in Publication Data

Main entry under title:
The Communications Handbook

Includes index.
ISBN 0-17-6015 07-8

1. Exposition (Rhetoric).
2. English language - Rhetoric.
3. English Language - Competition and exercises.
I. Goepfert, Paula S.

PE1429.C65   808'.042   C82-094288-X

1 2 3 4 5 6 7 8 9 0   8 8 7 6 5 4 3 2

TO THE STUDENT This book will answer your questions about a wide variety of everyday situations, both inside and outside the classroom: studying, writing exams, developing and presenting written assignments, making speeches and oral presentations, and many others. *The Communications Handbook* will be a useful reference in every school subject in which written or spoken communication counts. Keep it handy in your binder.

Using the Handbook

1. At the beginning of the year:

    *   Become familiar with the contents and organization of the book. Examine the Table of Contents and Index and then quickly skim each chapter. This will make it easier to locate specific material later on.

    *   Read all of Chapter 1: Study Skills. Its suggestions will be useful throughout the school year.

2. Before an assignment is submitted:

    *   Use the Index or Table of Contents to find the section related to the assignment. During the development stage, consult that section and any others that are appropriate to the topic.

    *   At this time, you might do the related exercises (entitled *Test Yourself*) to check and confirm your understanding of the Handbook material. *Note*: Answers to each exercise are provided at the back of the book.

    *   If a written assignment is involved, consult Chapter 4 to see that the proper format is used.

    *   After the final draft of an assignment is written, examine the Proofreading and Editing Checklist and related sections in Chapter 5 to see if there are any improvements that might be made before the final copy is submitted.

3. After an assignment is returned:

    *   The teacher may draw your attention to specific sections in the Handbook to point out ways of improving the assignment.

    *   When the teacher does this, reread the sections indicated. At this point, the *Test Yourself* exercises may also be completed in order to double-check your understanding.

THE COMMUNICATIONS HANDBOOK
Table of Contents

Chapter 6: LETTERS / 116

Chapter 7: LISTENING AND SPEAKING / 138

Appendix:

Preface

The Communications Handbook is intended to provide a practical and concise resource manual that secondary students at various levels can use for assignments in all subject areas.

In addition to providing a thorough resource for dealing with written work in terms of grammar, usage, mechanics, and format for all written assignments, the Handbook offers a number of other unique features:

- It provides guidelines for effective *listening and speaking* in specific situations inside and outside the classroom.
- It outlines the stages of *the writing process*, from prewriting to writing to rereading and revising, and it applies the process to all types of written assignments.
- It aids in improving *study skills* in the areas of assignments and examinations.
- It offers a selection of brief *self-help exercises*. These are intended for use on an independent basis for reinforcement and evaluation when the need arises. Many of them can be done without pencil and paper. Answers provided at the back of the book allow immediate feedback.

When introduced to students early in the year and used as a reference on a regular basis, the Handbook will save valuable time for teachers and students alike by assisting in independent learning. It will also encourage a common set of standards and practices across the curriculum.

CHAPTER 1
Study Skills

STUDY SKILLS

Are you making the best use of your time? Are
you looking in the right places for the information you need? Are your notes and outlines
really useful? Are you spending a lot of time
preparing for exams without the success you
expect? The tips you find in this Chapter may
make a big difference to you.

CONTENTS

ESTABLISHING PRIORITIES

Every day, you have more than one thing to do. You can usually organize your time by keeping a list of things to do and using it regularly to plan ahead. Making notes on a calendar is also very helpful. However, when you *do* get into last-minute problems, decide on your immediate priorities. Decide which of the many things you have to do should be done first. Ask yourself:

- Which is the most *urgent* (due today)?
- Which is the most *important* (counts for half the marks for the whole term)?
- Which is the most *personally important* (you care about it more than anything else)?

For Example:

You wake up one morning and realize that *tomorrow* you have a chemistry exam, a French quiz, and an essay due for your literature class. You *thought* you had planned ahead, but now it looks impossible.

Ask yourself some questions: "How important is the chemistry exam? How long do I need to study for it? Is it one of my good subjects?" Go through the same questions for the French quiz. Then review in your mind how much work you have already done on the essay.

Now set up a plan of attack. Here is how your reasoning might go:

- Chemistry exam very important; need all the time I can get; study for it for an hour after school to get an idea of where I need the most work, then study after dinner until I go to bed; exam first period of the day.

- French quiz just one of many this term; will do all right if I don't study; look at the material over lunch today for reassurance, then forget it till quiz time tomorrow; hope for the best.

- Literature essay three-quarters done; need to fix up the conclusion and recopy; make final touches to conclusion later this afternoon; recopy tomorrow during lunch; not due until last period tomorrow.

- Summary: Chemistry exam is the first priority; literature essay is the second priority but not as bad as I thought; French quiz will work out okay.

If you have seven things on your list and three are quick and easy, try to get the three easy things out of the way first. This way, you can almost cut your list in half. *But* do not put off the larger, more important tasks. Chip away at them steadily. Then they will become less "impossible" than they appeared to be.

KNOWING YOUR RESOURCES

Many times in the course of a school year, you will find it useful and even necessary to get help from someone or something. Find out who and what your resources are before you need them.

1. **The library:** Read *Using the Library, page 41.* Then learn to find your way around your own library.

2. **Teachers:** Get in the habit of asking your own or other teachers for advice on school work.

3. **Friends and family:** Do you have a friend who will explain logarithms to you if you proofread his or her English paper? Make an exchange.

4. **People in your community:** Most of them will probably be very happy to be interviewed if they have information that will help you. (See also *Interviews, page 146*.)

5. **Radio and television:** Watch for programs that relate to things you are studying in school. Take notes and write down the program, the name of the producer, and the date, time, and station on which the program was shown, so you can credit your source.

6. **Magazines and newspapers:** These publications are especially useful in obtaining up-to-date information. Clip articles out and file them.

7. **Businesses, public service organizations, and government departments:** These publish free pamphlets and information sheets for public distribution. Look up a list of government departments (provincial and federal) and see which is likely to have information pertaining to your project. Write or call *any* of the above resources to see what is available. Address your call or letter to "The Public Relations Department". (See also *Business Letters, page 123*.)

ASKING QUESTIONS

The habit of asking questions (and listening carefully to the answers) is an important skill.

Sometimes questions are the best way of getting information. For example, there is no point in spending an hour wandering around a large research library when there is an information desk and a person waiting to direct you to what you need.

Be specific and direct. If your question is vague, you will confuse the person you are asking and the answer you receive will probably confuse you.

Be persistent. If you do not get a good answer to your question the first time, rephrase it. For example, your teacher has just finished explaining an assignment due next week. You wonder if you have to write it in ink. You ask, "How are we supposed to do it?" Your teacher replies, "Do the best you can. Try the library and support your opinion." When this happens, rephrase the question. Say, "No — I mean, do you want the assignment written in ink?" You'll get your answer.

The SQ3R STUDY METHOD

How do you know what parts of a reading assignment are important to remember? How can you retain all of that information? The *SQ3R method**
of studying a book can point out the main ideas in a text and can also help you to remember them. SQ3R means Survey, Question, Read, Recite and Review. Here is how to use the five steps in the SQ3R method to read a chapter in a book:

*The SQ3R method of studying was developed by Francis P. Robinson, a psychologist from Ohio State University.

1. **Survey:** Quickly look over the headings in the chapter to see the few central points that will be developed. Then read the summary paragraph if the chapter has one. This survey should take a minute or two. It will reveal the four or five central ideas in the chapter and will help to organize those ideas.

2. **Question:** Turn the first heading into a question that has to be answered. It will bring to mind information that you already know and will also help you to understand that section more quickly. The question will also make main points in the section stand out, because they will be important in the answer to the question.

3. **Read:** Read the section under the first heading in order to answer the question. Be aware that you are making an *active* search for information.

4. **Recite:** Now that you have read the first section, put the book aside and try to answer briefly the question you asked earlier. Use your own words and try to give examples. If you can do this, you have learned the material. If you cannot, look over the section again. A good way to do this step is to jot down some key phrases, perhaps in outline form, on a sheet of paper.

Now repeat steps 2, 3, and 4 with each section of the chapter. Phrase each heading as a question, read the section to answer the question, and recite the answer to the question by writing down key phrases. Go through the whole chapter this way.

5. **Review:** When you have finished the chapter, glance over your notes to get an overview of the points and their relationship to one another. Check your memory of the content by stating the points under every heading. Do this by covering up the notes and trying to recall the headings. Then uncover each heading and try to recall the points listed under it.

These five steps of the SQ3R method should result in faster reading and help you to remember the important points in a reading assignment. You will also find that quizzes in class will be easier with this method, because the headings turned into questions are usually the points stressed in quizzes.

LEARNING TO SKIM MATERIAL

You are probably being asked to do a great deal of reading, especially for reports, essays, and exams. To read efficiently, it is important to learn to glance at some kinds of written material quickly and to read other kinds of material with concentration. You must also learn to judge which kind of reading is most appropriate to your purpose. This is developed by experimenting with both methods.

The way to get the most out of what you read in the shortest time period is to *skim*. This method will give you a general sense of the material you have to read and tell you whether or not the material is useful.

1. Carefully read the **title**. It gives a good idea of the subject matter.

2. Read through the **table of contents**. It will give a preview of the specific subjects covered in the book and of any special features, such as maps, tables, illustrations, or appendices.

3. Read the **preface, foreword,** or **introduction** to find out the purpose of the book.

4. Look at any **appendices** included at the back of the book. These contain basic reference materials that may be useful. For example, you may find a list of the prime ministers of Canada and their dates in office, a diagram showing the structure of the Canadian government, and so on.

5. Check to see if there is an **index**. It may help you to locate a specific piece of information later.

6. Check the **copyright page** (usually following the title page). It will tell you the date and place of publication. If you need very current information, the date of publication may tell you the book is too old, or the place of publication inappropriate for your purpose. For example, if you are writing a paper on automotive regulations in Canada today, and the book was published in London, England, in 1960, then you will know that it is not appropriate.

7. Finally, read the **chapter headings** and quickly flip pages to get the main ideas. Occasionally, read a small section that looks important. It may deal with what you really want to know.

MAKING NOTES

Nobody's mind can keep track of *all* the information it receives. Notes will help you:

- extend your memory
- organize your thoughts
- gather information
- learn new material
- review material
- summarize

Notes can be taken from many sources: books, lectures, speeches, or informational films.

General Tips

These hints apply whether the notes are taken from spoken or written sources.

1. Write your notes as **neatly** as possible and leave space between ideas. Then you will be able to read them later and perhaps add to them.

2. **Identify** your notes by writing down the date the notes were taken, the source (the title of the lecture or book, including the pages or sections covered), and the name of the subject to which the notes pertain.

3. Keep all notes for a single subject together and **in order** by date or topic.

4. Write notes **in your own words**. This technique forces you to think about what has been said or written by someone else.

5. **Be selective**. Write down only main ideas, important supporting ideas, and facts. Do not try to write down every word of an author or a speaker, or you will become confused.

6. **Symbols and abbreviations** are useful in note-taking. But if you get carried away, you will have to use valuable time translating your own notes just when you need them in a hurry.

Running Notes

You can take running notes, writing down the main ideas as they are presented. Try to include headings as a guide. For example, when taking notes on a speech, divide your notes into introduction and thesis statement, major topics covered in the body, and concluding remarks.

Whenever possible, take notes in outline point form. (See also *Using Lists and Outlines, page 12*.) This method organizes your material and thoughts as you go along.

When you are gathering information from books, you may wish to take notes by topic on individual cards. This system is especially well suited to research paper assignments. (See also *Taking Notes on Cards, page 48*.)

Underlining or Highlighting

If you are using a book that you own, you may wish to mark important sentences or passages. Do not consider underlining or highlighting a substitute for your own handwritten notes. When you underline, you may not really think about what you are reading, and you may not form clear impressions about the main idea(s) of a section.

USING LISTS AND OUTLINES

Lists are an informal method of keeping track of what you have to do and what you want to do. Outlines are formal organizational systems; they are indispensable in preparing to write an essay, a report, a research paper, or a speech.

Lists

All lists contain a line-by-line summary of things to do or remember or get. Here are some of the ways you can use lists in school:

1. In the first few weeks of school, make a master list for each of your classes that describes:

   - the **course requirements** (number of exams, projects, essays, assignments, and how much each counts toward the final grade)
   - your teacher's **special rules** (write exams and assignments in ink, points subtracted for late work, no typing allowed, and so on)
   - the **topics** the class will cover (cells, plants, measurement, matter, electricity, and so on)

   Attach each list to the inside front cover of the appropriate notebook or section in your notebook.

2. Regularly make a list of **things you must do**, especially when you feel pressured for time. Then use the list to establish your priorities. (See also *Establishing Priorities, page 8.*)

3. Make a list of **questions** to ask your teacher, if you have difficulty with a certain assignment or are very interested in it.

4. Keep a list of **vocabulary words** about which you are unsure, if you are reading a difficult book or article. When you have finished reading the material, look up the words in a dictionary.

Outlines

There are two kinds of outline. Entries in a *topic outline* are phrases, whereas entries in a *sentence outline* are complete sentences. Here is the format for both topic and sentence outlines:

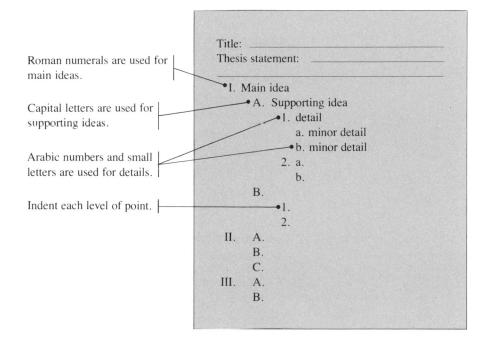

Roman numerals are used for main ideas.

Capital letters are used for supporting ideas.

Arabic numbers and small letters are used for details.

Indent each level of point.

Title: _____
Thesis statement: _____

I. Main idea
   A. Supporting idea
     1. detail
       a. minor detail
       b. minor detail
     2. a.
        b.
   B.
     1.
     2.
II. A.
    B.
    C.
III. A.
    B.

In general, use a topic outline when you are organizing a paragraph or simple essay. Use a sentence outline to prepare to write most essays, reports, speeches, and especially research papers. A sentence outline will force you to think each point through before you include it in your paper. (See also *Step 5, page 20.*)

EXAMINATIONS

Studying for the Exam

Here are some guidelines you may find helpful in preparing for an exam. Many of them apply to study habits in general.

1. Choose a **regular place and time** for studying. The place should be quiet and comfortable. The time should be carefully chosen so that your other activities and responsibilities will not interfere. Take regular breaks, but keep them short.

2. Start studying for an exam **several days before** the date it is scheduled, then review the material again the evening before. This plan gives you time to find out about something you may not know. It also makes the evening-before session more relaxed.

3. While studying, note the **main ideas** and organize the **details** and **examples** under these ideas. Also make note of any **questions** you will need to answer for yourself before the exam.

4. Select a number of **potential exam questions** and practise answering them in outline form. You might then choose one question and practise writing a full answer for it.

Writing the Exam

An exam may have many formats. It may include true-false sections, multiple-choice questions, short-answer questions, essay questions, problems, and so on. Here are some guidelines that apply to any type of exam:

1. **Make a quick survey of the entire exam**.

   - Look for specific directions, such as "Write in ink" or "Do all scratch work on the exam paper".

   - Try to get a sense of the overall length of the exam. Do you need to write every second or will you finish with time to spare?

   - Note what kinds of sections make up the exam, how many points are awarded for each, which sections you can do quickly, and which will take more time.

2. **Write neatly and clearly.**
   A *T* that looks like an *F* in a true-false section will be marked wrong. Also watch out for spelling and punctuation errors. If you have no idea how to spell a word that comes to mind, avoid using it; think of a word to replace it or rephrase the sentence.

3. **Carefully consider each question before you write.**

   - Look for key words in the question, such as *explain, compare, contrast, discuss,* and *define*.

   - Each of these key words tells you to do something different. Do only what the question asks, but do it completely and concisely.

   - Identify precisely what the question is asking and answer accordingly. If the question asks, "What is the quotient of $752.8 \div 27.62$, rounded off to the nearest hundredth?", you will not receive full credit for simply performing the indicated division. To be correct, you must round off your answer as instructed.

4. **Use a formal writing style for answers.**

   - Write all answers in full sentences unless instructed otherwise.

   - Paragraph and essay-type answers should follow a *thesis-proof-conclusion* format. This means the opening statements of the answer should clearly state your position or thesis. Next, give at least two specific examples, illustrations, or proofs of the thesis. Conclude with a summary of the points stated in general terms.

5. **Be concise.**
   You will probably need most of the time allotted to complete the exam. Therefore you must think before you answer, choose your words carefully, and resist any temptation to ramble or to pad your answers.

6. **Use your time wisely.**
   If you do not know the answer to a question or think that it will take a long time to produce, go on to the next question. Then return to the first question later.

7. **Check over your completed exam.**
   Make sure that you have answered everything that you can. Look for grammar, punctuation, spelling, and arithmetic errors, and any words that are unclear because of hurried writing. Write your name on each page.

CHAPTER 2
The Writing Process

PARAGRAPHS AND ESSAYS

Very rarely can anyone sit down and write a good essay on the first try. It takes planning -- and that is what the "writing process" is all about. Learning to write in an organized way will make every assignment less complicated and more effective. Find out about the eight steps to effective writing in this Chapter.

CONTENTS

SUMMARY OF THE WRITING PROCESS

There are three major stages in the writing process. They are prewriting, writing, and revising. To explain them in more detail, we can further divide them into eight steps — the eight basic steps in the writing process. Some or all of these steps are always used by good writers, whether they are writing fiction or nonfiction.

THE WRITING PROCESS

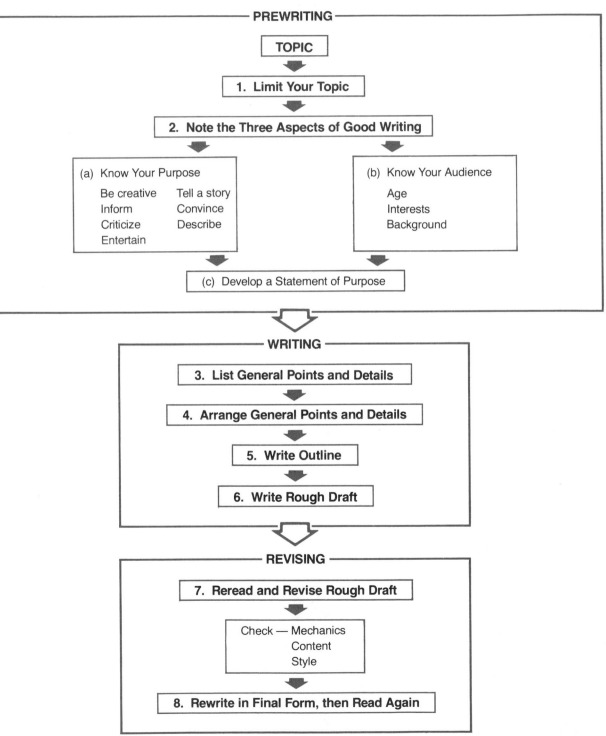

PREWRITING

TOPIC

1. **Limit Your Topic**

2. **Note the Three Aspects of Good Writing**

(a) Know Your Purpose

Be creative	Tell a story
Inform	Convince
Criticize	Describe
Entertain	

(b) Know Your Audience

Age
Interests
Background

(c) Develop a Statement of Purpose

WRITING

3. **List General Points and Details**

4. **Arrange General Points and Details**

5. **Write Outline**

6. **Write Rough Draft**

REVISING

7. **Reread and Revise Rough Draft**

Check — Mechanics
Content
Style

8. **Rewrite in Final Form, then Read Again**

PARAGRAPHS   A paragraph is a group of related sentences that develop one idea. Let's apply the eight steps of the writing process to an imaginary school assignment which requires one paragraph.

> Assignment: Write *one paragraph* about *an important decision* in *the settlement of the west.*

STEP 1: LIMIT YOUR TOPIC.

Begin by taking a close look at the directions for the assignment. Identify the *key words* in the directions. This is what they tell you:

(a) Chose a topic that can be effectively covered in *one paragraph.*

(b) Be certain that the topic is about an *important decision*, not just any decision.

(c) The important decision must be important in *the settlement of the west* as a whole, not simply important to a special region or group.

Next list several possible topics and jot down or mentally note your reaction to each one. Keep in mind the key words in the assignment.

Possible Topics:	**Possible Reactions:**
(a) decision to build the C.P.R.	too obvious; don't want to write about it; everybody else is
(b) decision by the federal government not to interfere with treason conviction of Riel in Regina	hard to cover in one paragraph; complicated
(c) decision to send settlers and establish government	too general; assignment presumes decision to send settlers
(d) decision to establish North West Mounted Police	allowed settlers to feel safe; solved many problems
(e) decision by "Laurier-Greenway compromise" to deny public financial support to separate schools in Manitoba	not directly related to settlement of west as a whole

Of the above possibilities, (d) seems to be the best. No immediate problems come to mind, so it certainly has potential. Quickly double-check your choice. Sometimes the best choice does not turn up in your first list of possibilities.

Double-check:

• Can I write effectively about this topic in one paragraph?
• Was the decision to establish the North West Mounted Police an important one?
• Was it essential to the settlement of the west?

If you can answer "yes" when you double-check, then you are ready for the next step in the writing process.

STEP 2: CONSIDER THESE THREE ASPECTS OF GOOD WRITING.

Three important aspects of good writing:

(a) Know your purpose.

(b) Know your audience.

(c) Develop a statement of purpose.

Always think through these three points before starting to write.

(a) **What is the purpose of developing this topic?**

Some possible purposes:

- to describe the organization of the N.W.M.P.
- to entertain the reader with stories about the N.W.M.P.
- to be creative
- to criticize
- to inform
- to tell a story
- to convince

Of the possible purposes we have listed, two stand out: *to inform* and *to convince*. They seemed to be implied in the assignment question by the word "important".

Purpose: to convince the audience, by providing information, that the decision to establish the N.W.M.P. was important to the settlement of the west

(b) **Who is my audience?**

- Mr. Eisner, Canadian Studies teacher
- will expect facts to support my opinion
- will expect good organization
- will expect good punctuation and spelling

Audience: Mr. Eisner, who expects supporting facts, good organization, and proper punctuation and spelling

(c) **Develop a statement of purpose.**
A statement of purpose combines what you have learned in *know your purpose* and *know your audience* into one sentence. As you continue to work on the assignment, this statement will tell you what to include in your paragraph and how to arrange your points.

Statement of Purpose: I am writing one paragraph in which I will use facts to convince Mr. Eisner that the decision to establish the N.W.M.P. was important to the settlement of the west.

STEP 3: LIST GENERAL POINTS AND DETAILS.

The next thing you need is information. Make a list of all the general
points and details about the topic. Then cross out (or put an X beside) the
points that do not relate directly to the purpose.

X Indians	— American Sioux flood Canadian Blackfoot territory after Custer's last stand
Settlers	— Government wanted to establish solid claim to territory
X Background	— Original North West Mounted Police is today's R.C.M.P.
Lawlessness	— Slideout, Robbers' Roost, Whiskey Gap, and Fort Whoop-Up smuggle U.S. liquor
Settlers	— Ottawa concerned over sovereignty because of involvement of U.S. smugglers
Background	— Sir John A. Macdonald establishes force in 1873
X Background	— Original recruits numbered 150
Lawlessness	— Murder and brutality commonplace
Lawlessness	— Man's life worth a horse; horse worth a gallon of whisky
Background	— If U.S. took over territory, access to west coast cut off
Settlers	— Without settlement American takeover of territory feared
N.W.M.P. (solution)	— N.W.M.P. establishes order in 7 years
X Background	— Original force headquartered at Fort Macleod

STEP 4: DECIDE HOW TO PRESENT AND ARRANGE POINTS.

Now that you have listed your information, you need to organize it. Choose
(a) a *style of presentation* and (b) a *method of arrangement* that suit your
idea, your information, and your purpose.

(a) Possible types of presentation:
- give facts
- use examples and illustrations
- relate specific incidents
- compare and contrast
- show cause and effect
- define
- give reasons or arguments

(b) Possible methods of arrangement:
- by time (chronologically)
- by importance or rank
- by location or place

How do you choose from all these possibilities? Take another look at the statement of purpose: "I am writing one paragraph in which I will *use facts* to *convince* Mr. Eisner that the decision to establish the North West Mounted Police was *important* to the settlement of the west." Then, cross out the styles of presentation and methods of arrangement that are not suitable for the purpose.

The best style of presentation for this particular example is to *give facts* and to *give reasons or arguments*. The best method of arrangement is to order the details according to *importance or rank*. This should convince Mr. Eisner that the decision to establish the North West Mounted Police was important.

STEP 5: MAKE AN OUTLINE.

An outline is a list of points in the order in which they will be presented in the assignment. It can be very general or very specific depending on whether the assignment is straightforward or complicated; for example, a paragraph or a research paper. An outline is essential for organizing every written assignment. (See also *Outlines, page 12*.)

In this example, we will use a topic outline as a plan for writing the rough draft.

Title: The North West Mounted Police in the West

Thesis Statement: The decision to establish the N.W.M.P. was important to the settlement of the west because people were afraid to settle in a lawless territory.

I. widespread lawlessness greatest problem
 A. murder and brutality commonplace
 B. places like Slideout and Fort Whoop-Up smuggle liquor
 C. man's life worth a horse; horse worth a gallon of whisky

II. Canadian government wanted to establish solid claim to territory
 A. U.S. smugglers caused concern over sovereignty
 B. possibility American settlers would follow and take over territory
 C. feared Canadian access to west coast would be cut off

III. North West Mounted Police was solution
 A. cleaned up west in 7 years
 B. settlement went forward and ensured Canadian claim to territory

STEP 6: WRITE A ROUGH DRAFT.

A rough draft is a first try. Referring to the outline, turn the points into sentences. Do not be too worried about minor details at this stage or you might get "writer's block". Use a pencil and double space so that revisions will be easier to make later.

Remember that the first line of every paragraph is indented and that all paragraphs contain a topic sentence, a body, and a conclusion.

Begin by writing a good topic sentence. It should tell the reader the main idea. The body sentences use details to support and develop the main idea. Conclude the paragraph with a sentence that summarizes the main idea. *Note*: This applies to informational writing only, not to fiction writing, in which various paragraph styles may be used for effect.

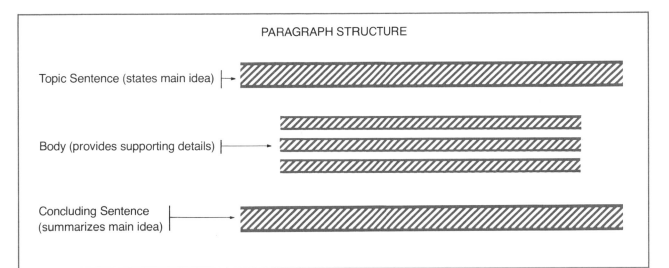

PARAGRAPH STRUCTURE

Topic Sentence (states main idea)

Body (provides supporting details)

Concluding Sentence (summarizes main idea)

STEP 7: REVISE THE ROUGH DRAFT.

Here is what to look for when you revise:

Content:
- inaccurate statements (if in doubt, recheck your sources)
- conclusions not supported by facts

Style:
- errors in grammar and sentence structure
- errors in word choice
- unclear sentences
- rambling sentences

Mechanics:
- spelling errors
- capitalization errors
- punctuation errors

When you think that there are no more content, style, or mechanical errors, ask yourself: *"Have I fulfilled the plan in my statement of purpose?"* If you cannot answer an instant "Yes", recheck to see if sentences are forcefully worded and if you have included all the necessary details to support your points.

On the next page is an example of one way to revise the rough draft of Step 6, using Step 7 as a guide.

A Crucial Decision
~~The North West Mounted Police~~

In 1873
Sir John A. Macdonald made the di~~i~~[e]cision ~~in 1873~~ to ~~start~~ [establish] the North West Mounted Police. This [decision] was ~~important~~ [crucial] to the [settlement of the] ~~West~~ because, before the [arrival of the] Mounties, few settlers ~~wanted~~ [were willing] to make [their] homes ~~there~~ [in the new territory]. The greatest problem was wide spread lawlessness. Murder and brutality were commonplace. Places like Slideout, Robber's Roost, Whiskey Gap, and, [most notorious of all,] Fort Whoop-Up ran a [brisk] business smuggling ~~in~~ liquor from the [United States] ~~U.S.~~ At these "whisky forts" it was said that a man's life was worth one ~~live~~ horse [and] a horse was worth a gallon of whisky. The [Macdonald] government wanted settlers in the West so it could [ensure its] ~~make sure it had a~~ claim to the [territory] ~~West~~. [At the time,] The whisky smugglers were considered a threat to [Canadian] ~~the~~ sovereignty ~~of the land~~ because the government was afraid American settlers would follow them [into the territory] and ~~take over the West~~ [claim it] for the [United States] ~~U.S.~~ ~~They were afraid~~ If that [had] happened, Canadian access to the [W]est [C]oast would have been cut off. The solution to these problems [proved to be] ~~was~~ the North West Mounted Police. [Within seven] ~~In 7~~ years [of the day] ~~from when~~ Sir John ~~A. Macdonald~~ [made the decision to] set up the force, the Mounties had cleaned up the whisky forts and stopped the smuggling. Only [after] ~~when~~ the Mounties brought law and order could the settlement of the [W]est begin and [the] Canadian claim to the land be firmly established.

STEP 8: PREPARE YOUR FINAL COPY.

In general, a finished assignment should follow this format:

(a) Put your name, the assignment name, your class or section, and the date on *each* piece of paper you hand in.

(b) Use clean, white paper, *not* paper torn from a spiral binder.

(c) Write in blue or black ink (or type if required).

(d) Leave a 3-cm margin on the right and left sides and at the bottom of each page.

(e) Write only on one side of the paper.

(f) Indent each paragraph.

(g) Be sure to follow any special directions the teacher has given.

Here is the finished assignment for Mr. Eisner's Canadian Studies class. If this were your paragraph, it would be ready to hand in *after* you had reread it one final time, looking for any errors that could easily be corrected at the last minute. Insert any changes neatly.

Hazel Silliker
Canadian Studies
Mr. Eisner
1982 01 10

A Crucial Decision

In 1873, Sir John A. Macdonald made the decision to establish
the North West Mounted Police. This decision was crucial to the
settlement of the west because, before the arrival of the Mounties,
few settlers were willing to make their homes in the new territory.
The greatest problem was widespread lawlessness. Murder and brutality
were commonplace. Places like Slideout, Robbers' Roost, Whiskey Gap,
and, most notorious of all, Fort Whoop-Up ran a brisk business
smuggling liquor from the United States. At these "whisky forts"
it was said that a man's life was worth one horse and a horse was
worth a gallon of whisky. The Macdonald government wanted settlers
in the west so it could ensure its claim to the territory. At the
time, the whisky smugglers were considered a threat to Canadian
sovereignty because the government was afraid American settlers
would follow them into the territory and claim it for the United
States. If that had happened, Canadian access to the west coast would
have been cut off. The solutions to these problems proved to be
the North West Mounted Police. Within seven years of the day
Sir John made the decision to set up the force, the Mounties had
cleaned up the whisky forts and stopped the smuggling. Only after
the Mounties brought law and order could the settlement of the west
begin and the Canadian claim to the land be firmly established.

ESSAYS An essay is a series of paragraphs that develop a topic and express the writer's viewpoint on that topic. Each paragraph has its own main idea, body, and conclusion, but at the same time, it is part of either the introduction, body, or conclusion of the essay. A new paragraph is started whenever a new idea is introduced.

Follow the same steps of the writing process to write an essay that you used to write a paragraph. Because writing an essay is usually more involved than writing a paragraph, there are a few extra points to consider. (See also *Sample Essay, page 25.)*

Outline Write an outline before starting on a rough draft. It will save time, assist in organization, and show where you may need to add or subtract material before you even start writing. (See also *Outlines, page 20.)*

Introduction and Conclusion A good introduction will tell the reader what to expect in the body of the essay and make him or her want to keep reading. A good conclusion will tie up all the information in the body of the essay and make the reader think he or she has read something informative and worthwhile.

Here are some suggestions for writing introductions and conclusions:

A Foolproof Plan
- Say what you are going to say.   (introduction)
- Say what you have to say.   (body)
- Say what you said.   (conclusion)

By following this plan, you make sure the reader gets your point. The introduction prepares the reader by saying, "This is my main idea and these are the points I will develop to support that main idea." The body of the essay carries out the promise given in the introduction. The conclusion makes a final clarification for the reader by saying, "As you can see, my main idea is really a valid one. You should now be convinced of my point of view."

Let's consider the following example.

Assignment: Write an essay on a scientific discovery made in the twentieth century.

---

1. **Introduction:**

Every day, someone in Canada owes a vote of thanks to Alexander Fleming, the Scottish biologist who revolutionized the field of medicine with his 1928 discovery of penicillin. First used extensively during World War II, this now common antibiotic cures many of the killer diseases of centuries past. Modern technology has put the drug in the hands of physicians who can prescribe it to their patients as easily as aspirin. Penicillin is truly deserving of its nickname, "the wonder drug", and we would shock our ancestors by the way we take it for granted.

2. Body:

By rereading the introductory paragraph, you can easily guess what points would be developed in the body of the essay. It would probably consist of three paragraphs:

- information on the actual discovery made by Fleming

- a survey of the diseases that penicillin is used to treat

- a brief survey of the availability, cost, and techniques of administering penicillin

3. Conclusion:

> The next time the doctor tells you that you have a strep throat and need to take penicillin, give a moment's thought to Alexander Fleming. Thank him for protecting you from the possible complications of strep throat, scarlet fever, rheumatic fever, kidney disease, meningitis, or encephalitis. Be grateful that your worries are over with the prick of a needle or a few days of tablets. You are among the millions of lucky people who have escaped serious illness or death, all because of an odd little mould that aroused the curiosity of a great scientist.

Sample Essay

The essay on the following page has been written according to the eight steps of the writing process.

> Assignment: Write an essay that presents a personal point of view on some aspect of contemporary life.

Notice that the writer of this essay has used a combination of *fact, analysis,* and *opinion* in an attempt to persuade the reader to adopt the writer's point of view.

The sources of all quotations, diagrams, figures, statistics, and important ideas that are not your own should be acknowledged with footnotes. (See also *Footnotes, page 54*.)

The Tyranny of Television

No one would dispute the profound effect that television has had upon modern society. It has invaded our homes and lives to such an extent that it is impossible to ignore. Unfortunately, its influence has been mainly negative. The increase in acts of crime and violence, the breakdown of the family and the passivitiy of our citizens all find their roots in this medium called television. An understanding of television's role in the creation of these problems is the first step toward a positive trend for our future.

Contrary to many arguments expressed by the television industry, there is no doubt that television breeds a violent society. Banner headlines routinely proclaim that juvenile crime is increasing at a frightening rate. According to an article in Maclean's magazine, a study showed that "by the time a child was fourteen, he or she had seen 11 000 television murders."[1] Now that "murder" is a staple of the daily diet of television viewing, the shock value of the word -- and the act -- has all but disappeared. Sounds of children at play are punctuated by shouts of "I'll kill you!" Recently, a television actor, who plays a New York City detective, was called to testify at a Flordia trial in which a fifteen-year-old boy was sentenced to life imprisonment for the murder of an elderly widow. The defence lawyer's plea was "not guilty by reason of insanity caused by television violence intoxication."[2] Still, the television industry ignores these signs. Furthermore, any attempt by the industry to control the violent content of its own programming is laughable. For example, warnings designed to alert parents to possible adverse effects from particular programs now precede such

----

[1] Susanne Zwarun, "Interviews with Television Violence Expert Dr. Gregory Fouts", Maclean's, 26 Dec. 1977, p. 4.

[2] Zwarun, p. 3.

programs. However, the television industry has discovered that these warning statements have the effect of increasing rather than decreasing the viewing audience. We can reasonably assume that these audiences are swelled by the very individuals for whom the programs have been deemed inappropriate.

With the intrustion of television into the home, traditional family activities have shifted in focus from the family to the "talking box". For example, the family dinner table was once the place for discussing and reporting the day's events. This activity is now a rarity. A teacher in New Jersey reports,

> I once took a survey of my first graders,
> ...only two of the twenty-two children ate
> dinner with their family without watching
> television. The other twenty either ate
> by themselves in front of the TV or had it
> at the supper table....[3]

Parents and children alike have turned their attention away from one another and immersed themselves in the passive, make-believe world of trite comedies, mindless game shows, and glamorized crime stories. The thoughts and feelings being communicated among family members have been reduced to "Turn to the other channel" and "Be quiet, I'm trying to watch television."

Television is here to stay. There is no denying that. However, with the significant influence that television now exerts upon today's social patterns, we must be very careful about how we use this powerful medium. If the television industry is to be concerned only with what sells, then the viewer must be ready to make discriminating choices. Choose your programs wisely. Let television serve you. Do not become a slave to your television set.

----

[3]New York Times, 7 Oct. 1974, p. 6, cols. 2-4.

2

PRÉCIS   A précis is a summary of a piece of writing. It should be about one-third the length of the original.

If you are asked to write a précis of an essay, your first step will be to read the essay carefully, at least twice, making notes of the main points and important details. Pay particular attention to the introduction and the conclusion. To write the précis, condense the essay by eliminating excess words and unimportant details. Listed below are some other useful devices in précis writing:

- Substitute a one-word synonym for a phrase.
- Omit unnecessary repetitions.
- Use a collective noun instead of a series; for example, you might write "people" instead of "men, women, and children".

Check your written précis for length. See that it accurately reflects the meaning and tone of the original before you hand it in.

A précis of the essay in the previous section might read something like this:

                    The Tyranny of Television

     The profound effect of television upon modern society is indisputable.
Unfortunately, this influence is largely negative, encouraging violent crime,
family breakdown, and a passive citizenry. An understanding of television's
role in these problems is the key to a better future.

     Though the industry denies it, television undoubtedly produces a violent
society. Headlines proclaim frightening increases in juvenile crime. For
children who watch television murders almost daily, murder loses its horror.
In a Florida court case, a fifteen-year-old boy was actually defended against
a murder charge on the grounds of "insanity caused by television violence".
Attempts by the television industry to control the violence in its programs
are pathetic. Warnings to parents that precede such programs simply increase
the audience.

     Activities in the home now centre on the television rather than on the
family. Mealtime discussions have given way to TV-watching, and family
members are more interested in television than in each other.

     Television is here to stay. We must learn to choose our programs wisely.
We must be the masters of this powerful medium, not its slaves.

ASPECTS OF STYLE

Good writers always decide what general style they will use before they begin to write. Style is the "how" of writing or speaking. Once you know *what* you want to say, you must decide *how* you will say it. The *how* (style) plus the *what* (content) equals the total impression a reader will get from your writing.

Any single aspect of style can be suitable in one piece of writing and totally unsuitable in another. Its suitability depends on your *purpose* and your *audience*. The style you would use to write to a close friend would be different from the style you would use to write a research paper.

If you were to receive an award for being voted the best math student, you would not write a speech that began like this:

Gee, guys, it's really great of you to give me this award. Wow!

Instead you would write something like this:

Ladies and gentlemen, thank you for giving me this award.

If you were writing to a younger brother who was away at summer camp, you would not begin:

I wish to inform you that our father desires to visit you this coming weekend.

Instead, you would write something like this:

Dad is coming to see you next weekend.

Neither of the first two examples is wrong. Neither, however, is suitable for the intended *purpose* and *audience*. Keep both purpose and audience clearly in mind every time you write.

Formal versus Informal

Here are two excerpts, each from a different work. Both are designed to introduce the books to which they belong. Notice the contrast in style.

1. From *The Oxford Companion to the Theatre*, Third Edition, edited by Phyllis Hartnoll.

> While thus limiting our range to the theatrical theatre, it has nevertheless proved impossible to ignore completely the sister arts of music, dancing, and design. Opera and Ballet, which have vast literatures of their own, have each been dealt with in a single article, as has Incidental Music in the Theatre. No attempt has been made to include individual composers, though a few librettists have short notes, as have some ballet-dancers and choreographers.

Characteristics of formal style:

- serious in tone
- factual
- impersonal
- strictly conventional in structure and vocabulary

2. From *Northeast Bicycle Tours* by Eric Tobey and Richard Wolkenberg.

Sure, we needed a lot of biking hours and detailed map-drawing to pull this book together. But, looking at it now, we've left out one ultra-important instruction: When to ignore the maps. The routes in themselves are fun and safe and, in lots of spots, beautiful. We planned it that way. But what we can't plan for is your sense of Lewis-and-Clark'ism, the expedition kind of feeling that bicycle touring lends itself to. That's why you've chosen the bike, for its self-contained autonomy, leaving you free to explore backroads and country towns, people and places you'd miss by whizzing down the interstates in a living room on wheels. What we're trying to tell you is that this conglomeration of routes and maps is really just a bunch of suggestions. Take off from them.

Characteristics of informal style:

- friendly in tone
- personal
- grammatical but with some deliberate use of colloquial language ("Sure", "ultra-important", "planned it that way", "lends itself to", "a bunch of", and contractions such as "can't", "we're", and so on)

Whether you are writing in a formal or an informal style, your objective is to communicate with your reader. Formal style does not mean "big" words and convoluted sentences; informal style does not mean slang and sloppy sentences. Both styles should be clear and meaningful.

As a general guideline:

- Write most school assignments in formal style.
- Write to friends and people your own age in an informal style.

Test yourself:

Which sentences below are written in a formal style? Which are informal? Why?

1. Many traditional musical forms, including jazz, gospel, and rhythm and blues, can be identified in the work of famous rock stars.

2. I really like rock music, but it's not the best thing in the world to listen to when you're trying to study.

3. From 1956 to 1963, Elvis Presley was the most popular performer of rock music. His fame was eventually surpassed by a British rock group that burst on the international music scene in 1961: the Beatles.

Diction Diction is the choice and use of words. Good diction means choosing words that express ideas as clearly and effectively as possible. If you were writing about a one-masted sailboat you might write:

> A west wind filled the boat's sails and quickly pushed it across the water.

However, it would be more effective if you wrote something like this:

> A west wind filled the sloop's sails and quickly pushed it across the lake.

While the first example is not wrong, *boat* is not as accurate or precise as *sloop,* and *water* is not as precise as *lake.* Choosing words with the most accurate and precise meanings will help make your ideas, and therefore your writing, clear and effective.

As a general guideline:

- Choose words with accurate and precise meanings.
- Consult a dictionary or thesaurus.

Transitions Make certain you develop *a sense of coherence* in your writing through the use of transitions. By being coherent, you help the reader to follow your train of thought and to see the relationships between sentences and between paragraphs. Here are four kinds of transitions:

(a) Use a **pronoun** that refers to a person or idea just mentioned.

Weak Morley Callaghan is probably Canada's best-known story writer. "Two Fishermen" illustrates an understanding of people that is both compelling and disturbing.

Strong Morley Callaghan is probably Canada's best-known story writer. *His* "Two Fishermen" illustrates an understanding of people that is both compelling and disturbing.

(b) Repeat a **key word**.

Weak *The Peking News* is the oldest newspaper in the world. It is over 1500 years old.

Strong *The Peking News* is the oldest *newspaper* in the world. In operation 950 years before the invention of movable type, the *paper* is over 1500 years old.

(c) Refer directly to a preceding idea by using a **synonym**.

Weak Our closest living relative is the chimpanzee. Studies can reveal a great deal about my Uncle Murray.

Strong Our closest living relative is the *chimpanzee*. Studies of this fascinating *creature* can reveal a great deal about my Uncle Murray.

(d) Use a **transitional expression**.

Weak   Kyle broke his ankle skiing and has to use crutches. He stood at the front of the room to give a speech in class yesterday.

Strong   Kyle broke his ankle skiing and has to use crutches. *Nevertheless,* he stood at the front of the room to give a speech in class yesterday.

Here is a list of some of the most common transitional expressions, arranged by category. Use good judgement in selecting words from these categories.

Cause and Effect
accordingly
as a result
because
consequently
since
therefore
thus

Addition
also, too
at the same time
besides
equally important
finally
further
furthermore
lastly
moreover
next
in addition

Comparison
by way of comparison
in a similar way
let us compare
likewise
similarly

Summary
from what has been said
in brief
in short
in summary
in conclusion
on the whole

Time
after a short time
afterwards
at length
finally
immediately
in the future
in the past
meanwhile
soon
subsequently
ultimately
at last
eventually

Place
beside
beyond
here
there
on the other side
opposite

Explanation
for example
for instance
incidentally
indeed
in fact
in other words
in particular
namely
specifically
that is

Contrast
although
at the same time
but
however
in contrast
in spite of
nevertheless
on the contrary
though

Purpose
for this purpose
for this reason
to this end
with this in mind

As a general guideline:

- Do not overuse any one type of transition in a single assignment.

- Avoid using transitions artificially. If two parts are not related in thought, no transition can really link them.

Test yourself:

Fill in the blanks with appropriate transitions. Some blanks can be correctly filled with several different expressions.

1. We tend to think of our sun as being unique. However, _____ is really just one of millions of stars in the universe.

2. Astronomers are beginning to unlock the mysteries of the universe. With each passing year, _____ equipment becomes more elaborate.

3. In 1969, the first men landed on the moon. _____, space travel will be possible for everyone.

4. Many constellations are named after the signs of the zodiac. These _____ are supposed to resemble the things their names describe.

Persuasive Writing

Persuasive writing tries to convince the reader to believe or do something. The writer may appeal to the emotions or to the mind to get the desired result. Persuasive writing is often used in advertisements to get the reader to buy a product or a service. It may also be used in essays and other types of writing to get the reader to accept a point of view.

The Opening

A piece of persuasive writing gives the writer's opinion about a topic. It often begins with a device to catch the reader's attention. Some of these devices include:

- a question ("Have you ever considered how many more books we would read if there were no television?")

- an unusual detail ("The range of Emily Dickinson's poetry is remarkable, considering that she lived an isolated life in the small town of Amherst, Massachusetts.")

- an exaggeration ("The whole world watched as the car reached the finish line.")

- a detail about the topic that is important or dramatic ("Louis Riel's life ended in the police barracks at Regina on 16 November 1885.")

- a strong statement of the main idea of the work ("Many food additives have been proven to be dangerous to our health.")

The Body

The writer then provides evidence to support the opinion that has been offered in the opening sentences or paragraph. Since almost all controversial issues have sound arguments on both sides of the question, a good persuasive writer tries to anticipate opposing viewpoints and provide counter-arguments along with the main points in the essay.

The Conclusion

A piece of persuasive writing usually ends by summarizing the most important details of the argument and stating once again what the reader is to believe or do.

Almost any newspaper will provide good examples of persuasive writing. Editorial page writers and columnists are experts at it. Many advertisements also offer fine models of persuasion. One example of a writer worth examining is Allan Fotheringham, whose columns appear in a number of Canadian newspapers as well as in *Maclean's* magazine.

As a general guideline:

- Have a firm opinion that you want your reader to accept.
- Begin with a device to get the reader's attention.
- Offer evidence to support your opinion and counter opposing views.
- Conclude with a restatement of what you want the reader to do or believe.

Variety

Variety is desirable in virtually every kind of writing. To achieve variety, you must pay attention to two points:

(a) *Word choice:* Select words that are precise, colourful, and interesting.

(b) *Sentence structure:* Compose sentences that are, in turns, long, short, simple, and complex.

Here is an illustration of what is meant by variety:

No Variety = **Boring**	The writer of the Sherlock Holmes stories was Sir Arthur Conan Doyle. Doyle was born in 1859. Holmes was born in 1887. Doyle was a doctor. He wrote to fill in time while waiting for patients. He wrote the Holmes stories and historical novels. He liked the historical novels better. He wrote Holmes' death so he could write more historical novels.
Variety = **Interesting**	The creator of the Sherlock Holmes stories was Sir Arthur Conan Doyle. Doyle was born in 1859, Holmes in 1887. By profession, Doyle was a doctor, yet apparently he had a slow practice, for in between seeing patients, he wrote not only the Holmes mysteries but also historical novels. Surprisingly, the infallible detective eventually bored his creator. Doyle killed off Sherlock to concentrate on his other writing.

Usually the best place to consider variety is at the *revision* stage of your writing. Look carefully at the words you have chosen and at the kinds of sentences you have written.

Variety should not be overdone. It is easier to rewrite simple prose to achieve some measure of variety than to rewrite complicated, artificial prose to achieve clarity.

As a general guideline:

- Variety in word choice, sentence length, and sentence structure is desirable for any purpose and any audience.
- Variety should not interfere with clarity.

Test yourself:

Here is a paragraph that is rather boring to read. See if you can make it more interesting by adding variety. You do not have to add any information.

> Frankenstein is one of the earliest and most famous horror story characters. He comes from a novel by Mary Wollstonecraft Shelley. She wrote her book about Frankenstein in 1818. Many movies have been made about Frankenstein. There is a big mistake in most of them. The monster is called Frankenstein in the movies. In the book, the person who makes the monster is called Frankenstein. The monster has no name.

Figurative Language

Figurative language for our purposes here will be confined to *simile* and *metaphor*. (See also *Mixed Metaphor, page 79*.)

1. A simile compares one thing to another by using the word *like* or *as*.

2. A metaphor describes a thing as something else in order to suggest a likeness.

Both of these devices can add interest, depth, and flair to a piece of writing. Here are some comparisons of literal (or factual) and figurative presentations of the same ideas.

Literal	At one billion, the population of China is *staggering*.
Figurative (simile)	Numbering one billion, the people of China seem *as numerous as blades of grass*.
Literal	During the 1912-16 Manitoba enfranchisement struggle, Nellie McClung *worked aggressively and tirelessly* in defence of her principles.
Figurative (metaphor)	During the 1912-16 Manitoba enfranchisement struggle, Nellie McClung *carried an unsheathed sword* in defence of her principles.

Be cautious and selective in your use of similes and metaphors. Think how different the mental picture would be if we were to describe Nellie McClung (in the above example) as carrying "a heavy club". Always make figurative expressions serve the needs of your thought, your purpose, and your audience.

As a general guideline:

- Use figurative language sparingly in school assignments.
- When you *do* use figurative language, make sure it fits the assignment and the style you have chosen for that assignment.

Test yourself:

Which phrases in the following sentences would you describe as figurative language?

1. For children, the venom of a black widow spider can be as deadly as arsenic.
2. Silk, spun by spiders for their egg sacs and webs, is used for cross hairs in certain optical instruments.
3. Spiders trap and then paralyze their prey by injecting venom. Next, these eight-legged vampires treat their victims with digestive juices and suck up their soft body tissues.

Euphemism

A euphemism is a word or phrase that names a thing in an indirect or mild way because the direct way is perceived as unpleasant or harsh.

Euphemisms can be good or bad, sensible or silly. Here are some euphemisms, matched with the plain English to which they refer:

laid to rest	=	buried
technical services specialist	=	lab technician
developing nations	=	poor countries
starter home	=	small house
misleading phrase	=	lie
golden age endowment	=	old age pension
military solution	=	war
preowned, reconditioned	=	used
leather-like	=	vinyl

Some of the above euphemisms could be used for the sake of kindness or diplomacy; others are plainly designed to hide the truth. Be aware of the distinction.

As a general guideline:

- Your writing for school assignments should be free of euphemisms.

Slang

Slang is a colourful word or phrase that takes on a special meaning and increased popularity for a short period of time. Slang is always changing and is frequently understood by special groups rather than by the general public. For these two reasons, it is not considered acceptable in formal writing. If you want to create an informal, popular, up-to-date impression with a particular essay or story, slang will help you to accomplish this purpose. But be careful. Never use slang if you think your meaning will be missed by the reader.

As a general guideline:

- Avoid slang in formal writing or in school assignments.

Cliché

A cliché is an overused expression. Most clichés began as new and clever phrases; they are now clichés because they were used so many times that they became old and boring. Clichés should almost always be avoided in writing and speaking.

Here are some clichés (they are also called *trite expressions*):

add insult to injury	in the long run
bright as a new penny	narrow escape
cool as a cucumber	red-letter day
easier said than done	slowly but surely
finishing touches	this day and age
good as gold	word to the wise

Sometimes a cliché is the quickest and easiest way of expressing a given idea. But *try* to be original. It will stimulate your own thoughts, improve your facility of self-expression, and impress and please your reader.

As a general guideline:

- Do not use clichés in writing or in speaking, unless you are doing so for effect.

Jargon

Jargon, in a broad sense, refers to the use of special terms or fancy phrases that hide meaning (or try to cover up lack of meaning). Here is an example of jargon that confuses the reader:

> Positive input into the infrastructure impacts systematically on the functional base of the firm in that it stimulates a concretization of meaningful objectives from a strategic standpoint.

Do you know what that sentence means? Probably not. Chances are the writer does not have anything to say but wants to sound authoritative. When something has been written in this mixed-up way, do not be intimidated; be suspicious.

As a general guideline:

- Avoid using jargon in school assignments.
- Be suspicious of it.

Affected Language

A piece of writing that is affected may combine many of the types of writing you should avoid; it may be wordy, trite, redundant, awkward, euphemistic, or full of jargon. This style of writing should be avoided because it is not the simplest, clearest way of stating an idea. A writer who uses affected language is more interested in sounding impressive than in making his or her point.

Affected   Inasmuch as the Canadian mode of expression is distinct unto itself, substantially influenced though it may be by British and American usage, it would seem to be a matter of instant and obvious logic to recognize that we must maintain, in earnest, a system of orthographic conventions that is both nationalistic and appropriate to our individualistic heritage.

Unaffected   Although Canadian English has been influenced by British and American usage, Canadians should try to maintain a spelling system that is distinctly their own.

Affected style is not impressive. What is always sure to impress a reader is sensible, clearly presented thinking.

As a general guideline:

- Have something to say and say it in the simplest, clearest way you can.

A WRITING CHECKLIST

1. **Do I understand the assignment** (identified the key words)?

2. **Have I followed the eight steps of the writing process?** (*See page 16.*)

3. **Have I written effectively?**

   - Written in a style suited to my purpose and my audience?
   - Composed a solid topic sentence, a strong introduction, and a strong conclusion?
   - Used meaningful transitions so that the reader can follow my train of thought?
   - Made the overall piece interesting through careful word choice, sentences of varied lengths, and effective constructions?
   - Stuck to the point so that every sentence relates clearly to the main idea?

4. **Have I revised thoroughly?**

   - Checked the structure and content of each sentence and each paragraph, making sure that I have chosen the most effective way of stating my points with the most precise words?
   - Corrected all mechanical errors — spelling, punctuation, and capitalization?
   - Made sure I fulfilled my statement of purpose?
   - Made sure I fulfilled the requirements of the assignment?

5. **Have I prepared a polished copy?**

   - Followed the teacher's instructions for format and identified my paper clearly?
   - Used ink and clean paper, written on one side only, kept careful margins, and indented each paragraph?

6. **Have I reread my polished copy before handing it in?**

CHAPTER 3
Research Papers

RESEARCH PAPERS

Suppose you have a thousand-word research paper due in six weeks. Where do you start -- by sitting down to write the first paragraph, by making an outline, by visiting the library? A research paper is always a lot of work, but doing it systematically will help make the work easier and result in a more effective paper.

CONTENTS

A research paper is an essay in which you incorporate your own thoughts with other people's words and thoughts *and* give credit to those people. It is usually formal in style. Its purpose can be to inform or explain, to present a new point of view, or to present research findings. Two special skills are needed in order to write a proper research paper.

1. You have to be able to use the library efficiently.
2. You have to know how to document and present your research.

APPLYING THE WRITING PROCESS

The steps to follow in writing a research paper are identical to those in the general writing process (See also *The Writing Process, page 16*.) However, the work in three of these steps is slightly expanded in the research paper. Here is an overview of how to write a research paper:

STEP 1:   Limit your topic.

In a research paper, this step is performed *after* the preparation of a *preliminary bibliography*. (See also *Preliminary Bibliography, page 46*.)

STEP 2:   Consider these three aspects of good writing:

(a) Know your purpose.

(b) Know your audience.

(c) Develop a statement of purpose.

STEP 3:   List general points and details.

In a research paper, this step comes *after* you have carried out the research. You must *take notes* on your resource material so that you will be able to organize the points and details in your paper. (See also *Taking Notes on Cards, page 48*.)

STEP 4:   Decide how to present and arrange your points.

STEP 5:   Write an outline.

STEP 6:   Write a rough draft.

STEP 7:   Reread and revise.

STEP 8:   Prepare your finished copy.

In a research paper, you must now finalize your *footnotes*, your *bibliography*, and any *figures* you have included, and prepare them for submission with your paper in a polished form. (See also *Research Papers, page 54*.)

Before you begin to work your way through this process, you have to be able to find your way around the library.

USING THE LIBRARY

Library resources can be divided into four categories:

- books in the stacks
- reference books
- magazines and newspapers
- special resources (which vary considerably from one library to the next)

Books in the Stacks

1. **What to Expect**

Most of the books in a library are "in the stacks" (on open bookshelves). These books can be either fiction or nonfiction. You will be using mostly nonfiction books in a research paper.

A book in the stacks may cover a very broad area or it may be very narrow in scope. Generally speaking, the broader the area, the less detailed the information. For example, if you see two books of about the same size, one entitled *A History of the British Isles: From the Earliest Times to the Present* and the other called *Wales in the Twentieth Century*, the first book will have less information on Wales than the second.

Checking the dates of publication of books in the stacks is important. The information in most books is at least one year old. If up-to-date information is needed, a book copyrighted in 1960 would only be useful for background information.

Books can usually be borrowed from the stacks. However, be selective about what you check out. If you take too many books at one time and do not choose them carefully, the result can be hopeless confusion.

2. **How to Find What You Need: The Card Catalogue**

The card catalogue is a large cabinet filled with little drawers containing at least one card for every book in the library. A book in the library may be listed on three kinds of cards: (a) a *title* card, (b) an *author* card, and (c) a *subject* card. Larger libraries may have a separate cabinet for each of these three types of cards.

All the cards are arranged alphabetically. If you wanted to find the card for a book entitled *History of Modern Theatre*, you would look in the *title cabinet* under *H*. If you wanted to find a book by Ernest Hemingway, you would look in the *author cabinet* under *H*. If you wanted to find a book about harpoons, you would look in the *subject cabinet* under *H*.

The location of a book in the library is specified by the call number, given in the upper left-hand corner of the card. Nonfiction books in the stacks as well as reference books are arranged by these numbers (plus a letter coding), usually according to the *Dewey decimal system*. This system arranges books by category. For example, books in the category of religion have call numbers from 200 through 299; books in the category of the social sciences have call numbers from 300 through 399.

Here are examples of the three kinds of cards found in the card catalogue:

a) The *Title* Card:

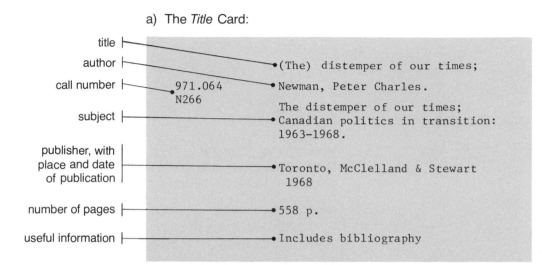

title ⊢

author ⊢ ●(The) distemper of our times;

call number ⊢ ● 971.064 ●Newman, Peter Charles.
N266

The distemper of our times;
subject ⊢ ●Canadian politics in transition:
1963–1968.

publisher, with
place and date ⊢ ●Toronto, McClelland & Stewart
of publication 1968

number of pages ⊢ ●558 p.

useful information ⊢ ●Includes bibliography

(b) The *Author* Card:

```
            Newman, Peter Charles.
971.064     The distemper of our times;
N266        Canadian politics in transition:
            1963-1968.
            Toronto, McClelland & Stewart    1968
            558 p.
            Includes bibliography
```

(c) The *Subject* Card:

```
            Politics and Government -- 1963-1968.
971.064     Newman, Peter Charles.
N266        The distemper of our times;
            Canadian politics in transition:
            1963-1968.
            Toronto, McClelland & Stewart    1968
            558 p.
            Includes bibliography
```

Reference Books

1. What to Expect

Reference books give factual information, free from opinion. They are a good source of background and summary material, but usually do not provide the most up-to-date information.

The material in reference books is often arranged alphabetically by subjects or key words; however, it may be arranged chronologically or topically.

Books in the reference section may not be removed from the library.

2. Where to Find Reference Books

Reference books are not hard to find. When you see the abbreviation "Ref." (for Reference) listed with the call numbers on the card in the card catalogue, you will know you have the card for a reference book. All reference books are located in the reference section of the library, according to their call numbers.

3. Some Useful Reference Books

- Dictionaries

    Concise Oxford Dictionary of Current English

    Dictionary of Canadian English: The Senior Dictionary

    The Oxford English Dictionary (This is a dictionary of thirteen volumes. It follows the British custom in spelling and pronunciation, which is closer to the Canadian custom than is the American.)

    Webster's Third New International Dictionary (This is a dictionary of one volume that follows the American custom of spelling and pronunciation. The latest edition of this dictionary is considerably more recent than the Oxford dictionary listed above.)

- Biographical Dictionaries

    Current Biography

    Macmillan Dictionary of Canadian Biography

    Who's Who (There are *Who's Who* books for international, Canadian, British, and American figures.)

- General Encyclopedias

    Collier's Encyclopedia

    Encyclopaedia Britannica

    Encyclopedia Canadiana

    World Book Encyclopedia

- Almanacs and Yearbooks (issued annually)

    Canada Year Book
    Canadian Almanac and Directory
    The People's Almanac
    World Almanac

- Atlases and Gazetteers

    Canadian Oxford Atlas of the World
    Columbia Lippincott Gazetteer of the World
    Historical Atlas of Canada
    National Geographic Atlas of the World
    Webster's Geographical Dictionary (a gazetteer)
    World Book Atlas

Note: A historical atlas shows areas as they were at a particular time in history. A gazetteer gives brief historical information about various places and provides a pronunciation guide.

- Quotations

    Bartlett's Familiar Quotations
    Colombo's Canadian Quotations
    The Oxford Dictionary of Quotations

- Magazine and Newspaper Indexes

    Canadian Periodical Index
    Index to The Times (London)
    Readers' Guide to Periodical Literature
    The New York Times Index

- History References

    Cambridge Ancient History
    Cambridge History of the British Empire
    Cambridge Medieval History

- Literature and Drama References

    Literary History of Canada
    The Oxford Companion to Canadian History and Literature
    The Oxford Companion to English Literature
    The Oxford Companion to the Theatre
    The Reader's Encyclopedia

- Philosophy and Mythology References

    A Handbook of Greek Mythology
    Larousse World Mythology
    The Encyclopedia of Philosophy

- Music and Art References

    Encyclopedia of World Art
    Grove's Dictionary of Music and Musicians
    The New Oxford History of Music

- Science and Technology References

    Applied Science and Technology Index
    A Dictionary of Geology
    The Encyclopedia of the Biological Sciences
    The Environment Index
    McGraw-Hill Encyclopedia of Science and Technology

Use the card catalogue and take advantage of these and other reference books that are available on your subject.

Magazines and Newspapers

1. **What to Expect**
   Most libraries keep a selection of magazines and newspapers. Magazines are called *periodicals*; newspapers are sometimes referred to by this term as well. In magazines and newspapers you can find up-to-date information on any topic. However, keep in mind that many magazine and newspaper articles are a combination of fact and opinion. Distinguish carefully between the two types of information.

2. **Where to Find Magazine Articles**
   If you wish to see what magazine articles exist on your topic, consult either the *Canadian Periodical Index* or the *Readers' Guide to Periodical Literature*. Both of these are found in the reference section of the library.

   Most libraries have a periodical desk at which you can check a listing of the magazines and newspapers available. At this desk, you will usually fill out a form stating the specific magazine you wish to see and the librarian will get it for you. Some libraries have bound copies of magazines on the shelves of the reference section.

3. **Where to Find Newspaper Articles**
   Certain newspapers, such as *The Times* (London) and *The New York Times*, have their own indexes. If you are interested in making a search of newspaper articles, ask your librarian what resources are available at your library.

   Most libraries will not allow you to remove magazines or newspapers from the premises.

Special Resources

Every library has "special resources". You will have to learn what special resources are available at your own library, but here are some possibilities:

1. **An Information File**
   This is a filing cabinet or box containing pamphlets generally arranged alphabetically by subject. These pamphlets may be issued by government departments, companies, professional groups, universities, or individual concerns.

2. **A Vertical File**
   This is a filing cabinet containing pictures and clippings from newspapers and magazines. These are arranged alphabetically by subject.

3. **Audio-Visual Materials**
   Phonograph records, cassettes, filmstrips, films, and multimedia kits are among the possibilities in this category. A card in the card catalogue may direct you to one of these resources, or a special cataloguing system may be used for them.

PRELIMINARY BIBLIOGRAPHY

A preliminary bibliography is a list of all the books, magazines, newspapers, and special resources that contain material related to your topic.

Preparing It

Let's prepare a preliminary bibliography for an imaginary school assignment.

> Assignment: Write a *research paper* about *one aspect of the structure of the Canadian government.*

You might begin by going to the card catalogue and looking under *Canada, Government, Politics,* and *British North America Act.*

For each card in the catalogue that seems to deal with the structure of the Canadian government, make your own 7 cm × 13 cm (3″ × 5″) file card, one card per book or resource. Copy the information from the card catalogue *exactly*. These cards are your preliminary bibliography.

Using It

A preliminary bibliography should be your guide in limiting your topic and preparing a rough outline. It should give *direction* to your research. Here is how to make it do that:

1. **Survey each resource for which you have made a card.** Find the resource listed on each card and spend a few minutes determining what it has to offer.

   - *Check* the table of contents, the date of publication, and the index.
   - *Scan* the potentially relevant sections.
   - *Note* whether the information is general or detailed, or accompanied by charts, graphs, maps, or other illustrations. You may wish to make some general notes on your bibliography card.

2. **Use the preliminary bibliography to limit your topic.** Ask yourself two questions:

- What areas are well covered in the resource materials I have surveyed?
- Of the materials covered, which are both significant and interesting?

Let's say that you decide to write about the role of the Senate. You might decide to pose a question and write an analytical paper. In that case, your topic could be, "Does the Senate contribute to the effectiveness of the federal government?"

Once you have limited your topic, make a quick readjustment of your preliminary bibliography. Put aside any cards not related to your specific topic (but save them, as you might find later that you need one or two of them). Now see if the remaining cards offer sufficient material. If not, you might go back to the card catalogue and look up *Senate*, *House of Commons*, and *Parliament*.

ROUGH OUTLINE

Using your preliminary bibliography and your findings from your survey of resources, make a rough outline of the points you will cover in the body of your paper. This outline will serve as a guide to your research. When your research has been completed, the rough outline may be revised to become your final outline. The final outline will be the guide to writing the paper.

In order to prepare a rough outline, ask yourself questions about the topic you have chosen. These questions might include who? what? when? where? how? why? Not all of these questions will apply to any one topic.

Topic: Does the Senate contribute to the effectiveness of the federal government?

I. Background—evolution of the Senate

II. Description of the Senate
   A. Composition
   B. Powers

III. Real contributions of the Senate
   A. Legislative
   B. Representative
   C. Advisory

IV. The Senate as a political force

V. Suggestions for new directions for the Senate

TAKING NOTES ON CARDS

Using your preliminary bibliography cards and your rough outline, you can now begin to gather detailed information. This means taking notes. If you have many resources to cover and are planning a complex paper, put your notes on cards — one piece of information per card. Here is how to do it:

1. Read the relevant material in each resource you have chosen.

2. Put the author's name and the title (in a shortened form) in the upper left-hand corner of each card you make.

3. Place only *one* piece of information or one quotation on each card. Include the page number(s) where you found the information.

4. Strive to take notes in your own words. (This method forces you to think about the material as you go along.)

5. If you would like to use a piece of information as a direct quotation in your paper, copy it down *exactly* and enclose it in quotation marks.

6. It is useful to make "idea cards" as you do your research. Idea cards can contain your own observations about the material and your interpretation of specific points.

Here is an example of a note card:

subject relative to rough outline

author and title (shortened form)

Dawson, <u>Gov't of Canada</u>   Power
The fact that the cabinet is responsible to the House of Commons and <u>not</u> to the Senate is indicative of power distribution in Parliament as a whole.

p. 280

information in your own words (Enclose direct quotations in quotation marks.)

page where information found

FINAL OUTLINE

If you have put only one piece of information on each card, you will be able to arrange the cards according to your outline. After you have gathered all your information, make a final outline of the paper (Step 5 of the writing process). Use the final outline as a guide to organize and write the paper.

Here is one version of a final outline based on the rough outline. (See also *Rough Outline, page 47*.)

Topic: Does the Senate contribute to the effectiveness of the federal government?

  I. Background — Evolution of the Senate

   A. Colonial period, Constitution Act/Canada Bill (1791)
   B. Confederation (1867)
   C. Statute of Westminster (1931)

 II. Description of the Senate

   A. Composition

     1. Reasoning behind composition rules (and rules)
     2. Composition today, by province and party

   B. Powers
     1. Legislative
     2. Representative
     3. Advisory

   C. Traditional or ceremonial considerations

III. Real contributions of the Senate

   A. Legislative — only minor changes in bills
   B. Representative — often nonpartisan character
   C. Advisory — recent activities of the Senate

 IV. The Senate as a political force

   A. Attempts to use the Senate as a political tool
   B. Senate value in defusing differences between provinces

  V. Suggestions for new directions for the Senate

PLAGIARISM

At each stage of the planning, note-taking, writing, and polishing of your paper, guard against *plagiarism*. Plagiarism is using someone else's words *or ideas* as if they were your own.

To prevent plagiarism:

- Use your own words.

- Use quotation marks any time you use someone else's words.

- Footnote any phrases or ideas that are not *completely* your own. (See also *Footnotes, page 54*.)

A RESEARCH PAPER CHECKLIST

A research paper presents a great deal of information, gathered from a variety of sources. This information will not be useful or interesting to your reader unless *you*, the writer, bring it all together to focus on a single, specific topic. This process is the most challenging aspect of writing a research paper. Here is a checklist to help you stay organized as you go along:

1. Have I followed the eight steps of the writing process?

2. Have I used the library and all other likely sources efficiently to gather all relevant information for my topic?

3. Have I documented all quotations, ideas, and information gained through research?

4. Have I accomplished my purpose?

5. Have I followed the correct format for presentation of a research paper? (See also *Research Papers, page 54.*)

Test yourself:

1. All libraries have several different kinds of resource material available. These are usually divided into books in the stacks, _____, _____, and special resources.

2. Imagine that you have been asked to write a research paper and that you have chosen "Houdini: The Greatest Escape Artist" as your topic. Your librarian tells you that you will find good background information in a book called *The Illustrated History Of Magic* by Milbourne Christopher. You look in the card catalogue at your library to find the book. What are the three ways the book will be listed and how could you find the book using each of the three ways? Which way would probably be the quickest in this case?

3. What two books would you consult to see if there had been any recent magazine articles on Houdini or other escape artists?

4. Here is an example of a note card that you might make for your paper on Houdini. What is missing? Why is the missing information important?

> Christopher, *Illustrated History of Magic*
>
> "Almost half a century after his last performance, Houdini's is still the best known name in magic."

5. Look back at the note card in question 4. Assume that you do use the information in the card, but not in the form of a direct quotation. You write instead, *Of all the many magicians past and present, Harry Houdini is still the greatest name in magic for most people today.* Should you footnote this sentence, written in your own words? Why or why not?

CHAPTER 4
Presenting Written Work

PRESENTING WRITTEN WORK

You are planning your assignment and need to make some decisions: Will it need footnotes and a bibliography? Will graphs or diagrams help? Are a Table of Contents page and Title page necessary? If so, how should they be done? Proper format is important for any assignment.

CONTENTS

The sections in this chapter explain the formats for regular assignments, essays, research papers, reports, and scientific papers. If, after reading this chapter, you are still uncertain about how to present a specific piece of writing, ask your teacher.

ASSIGNMENTS

Assignments are *everything* you turn in to the teacher: math problems, answers to questions, paragraphs, diagrams, and outlines. Every assignment should fit this description:

- It is neatly and clearly written.
- It has a 3-cm margin all the way around.
- The paper is clean and white, *not* paper torn from a spiral notebook.
- Except for math and science problems, it is written in blue or black ink.
- The writing is on one side of the paper only.
- Each page of the assignment is clearly identified with your name, your class, your teacher's name, the assignment title, and the date. (It may be acceptable to identify the pages after page one with only your name and the date.)
- If the assignment is more than one page long, all pages are clearly numbered and stapled.
- Each paragraph is indented.
- All specifications made by your teacher are carried out precisely.

PARAGRAPHS AND ESSAYS
Titles

To get an idea of what paragraphs and essays should look like on a page, see the sample paragraph on page 23 and the sample essay on page 26.

All paragraphs and essays should be titled. Here is how to present the title:

- Capitalize all important words.
- Do not use a period at the end. Use other punctuation as necessary.
- Do not underline the title.
- Place the title either on the first page of the essay or on a separate title page. The teacher may request one or the other, or may accept either.

1. **First page**

   If you put the title on the first page:
   - Put your name and all other identifying information in the upper right-hand corner.
   - Centre the title at the top of the page.
   - Leave one line between the title and the first line of the essay (or paragraph).

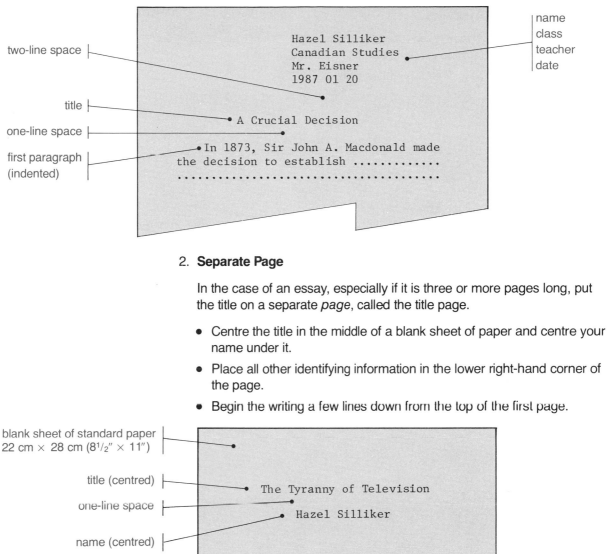

two-line space

title

one-line space

first paragraph (indented)

name
class
teacher
date

Hazel Silliker
Canadian Studies
Mr. Eisner
1987 01 20

A Crucial Decision

In 1873, Sir John A. Macdonald made
the decision to establish ....
....

2. **Separate Page**

In the case of an essay, especially if it is three or more pages long, put the title on a separate *page*, called the title page.

- Centre the title in the middle of a blank sheet of paper and centre your name under it.
- Place all other identifying information in the lower right-hand corner of the page.
- Begin the writing a few lines down from the top of the first page.

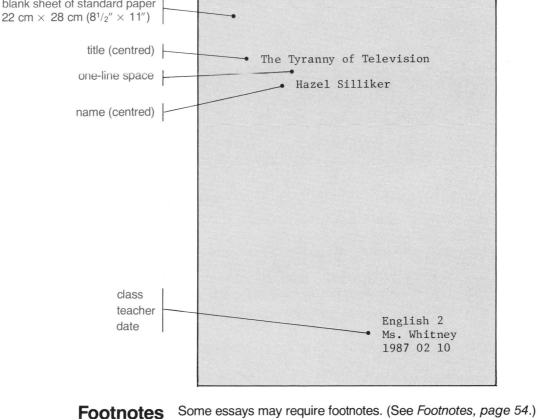

blank sheet of standard paper
22 cm × 28 cm (8¹/₂″ × 11″)

title (centred)

one-line space

name (centred)

The Tyranny of Television

Hazel Silliker

class
teacher
date

English 2
Ms. Whitney
1987 02 10

Footnotes   Some essays may require footnotes. (See *Footnotes, page 54.*)

RESEARCH PAPERS

This section will cover the presentation of a research paper. The distinguishing characteristics of a research paper are:

- It has a formal style.
- It has a title page.
- It includes footnotes and a bibliography.

Some research papers may also contain:

- a table of figures
- appendices
- a table of contents

Scientific papers based on experimentation and data collection follow a slightly different pattern. (See *Scientific Papers, page 63*.)

Title Page

The title page of a research paper is identical to the title page of an essay. (See *Titles, page 52*.)

Table of Contents

A table of contents should be included in a research paper if there are several sections with specific headings.

The table of contents should be placed immediately after the title page.

Here is a sample table of contents:

Footnotes

Footnotes are used for two purposes:

- to give credit to sources from which *quotations, diagrams, tables, statistics, numbers,* or *ideas* in the text of your paper were obtained
- to provide additional information or comments

Footnotes can be placed in one of two spots:

- at the bottom of the page where the notation occurs
- listed in numerical order, just before the bibliography (Do this if there are more than ten footnotes in the entire paper.)

1. Footnotes to Credit Sources

When you need to provide a footnote for material in your paper, place a superscript number (written in a raised position, such as the number 1 in the example below) directly following the material you are footnoting. Use this same superscript number to begin the footnote.

a notation within the paper

a line separating the footnote from the rest of the paper

a footnote

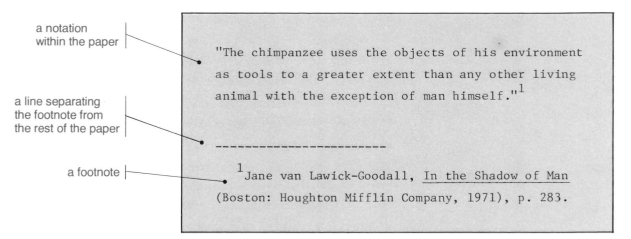

"The chimpanzee uses the objects of his environment as tools to a greater extent than any other living animal with the exception of man himself."[1]

————————————

[1] Jane van Lawick-Goodall, In the Shadow of Man (Boston: Houghton Mifflin Company, 1971), p. 283.

Here is an overview of the format used for footnotes.

- All footnotes are indented on the first line and single-spaced.
- Most footnotes begin with the author's name (first name first).
- Next comes the title of the work. Titles of articles or chapters are in quotation marks, not underlined. Books or magazine titles are underlined without quotation marks.
- Next, in parentheses, is the publication information. This information includes the place of publication, the publisher, and the date of publication.
- Lastly comes the exact page(s) where the material was found.
- Subsequent references for a source are usually given in a shortened form (See also *page 56*.)

Here is a standard footnote:

superscript number | author | comma | title | parentheses | place of publication | colon

[1] Margaret Atwood, Lady Oracle (Toronto: McClelland and Stewart Limited, 1976), p. 95.

publisher | date of publication | comma | page number of reference | period

Here is a series of examples, showing how to footnote different kinds of sources:

(a) Sources Used for the First Time

- A book with one author or editor

    [1]Bernice Jones, New Guide to Mountain Climbing (New York: Viking, 1957), p. 62.

    [2]Martin Sinn, ed., Mountain Building (London: Doubleday, 1978), p. 37.

- A book with two authors or editors

    [3]Allan Pressman and Paul Hamilton, Glaciers (Toronto: Dent, 1974), p. 102.

- A book with three or more authors or editors

    [4]Allan Bennett et al., Electrons on the Move (New York: Walker, 1964), p. 24.
    (et al. is an abbreviation for the Latin et alii, meaning "and others".)

- A work in a collection by several authors, with an editor

    [5]Robert Service, "The Cremation of Sam McGee," in Canadian Literature: The Beginnings to the 20th Century, ed. Catherine M. McLay (Toronto: McClelland and Stewart Limited, 1974), pp. 412–15.

- A book that has been translated

    [6]Fyodor Dostoyevsky, Crime and Punishment, trans. Sidney Monas (New York: The New American Library, 1968), p. 269.

- An article with an author's name listed from a magazine, periodical, or encyclopedia

    [7]William Bouche, "Climbing Gear," The Mountaineer, July 1972, p. 50.

    [8]Simon R. Hertzog, "Glaciation," Encyclopaedia Britannica, 1974 ed., Vol. 9, p. 47.

- A book or article with no author given

    [9]New Guide to Mountain Climbing, 5th ed. (New York: Viking, 1957), p. 62.

    [10]"Climbing Gear," The Mountaineer, July 1972, p. 50.

(b) Sources Used More Than Once

- If a source was footnoted earlier, you can use a *shortened footnote*, providing only the author's surname and the reference page number.

    [11]Jones, p. 203.

- When two or more books by the same author are used as reference material *or* there are sources by two or more authors with the same last name, include the title or an abbreviated form of it.

    [12]Jones, New Guide, p. 217.

- To refer to a source *immediately preceding*, some writers use the word *Ibid.* (an abbreviation for the Latin word *ibidem*, meaning "in the same place").

    [13]*Ibid.*

    If the page number is different, use *Ibid.* plus a comma and the correct page number.

    [14]*Ibid.*, p. 14.

    Note: Ibid. is no longer commonly used. (See also *Abbreviations, page 59*.)

2. **Footnotes to Provide Additional Information**
   Sometimes a writer wishes to use a footnote to provide extra information that is not appropriate to include in the body of the paper. Extra information may include a minor research point, additional observations, or background information that will aid the reader in understanding the topic or process being described.

   This kind of footnoting should be used rarely. Usually, if information is not worth including in your text, it is not worthy of a special footnote.

Checklist for Footnoting

Have I:

1. Placed the appropriate footnote number at the end of the quotation or material being noted?

2. Raised the number above the line?

3. Numbered the notes consecutively?

4. Indented the first line of each note?

5. Checked punctuation in the notes?

6. Reproduced all the necessary information in the notes *exactly* from the original source?

Bibliography

A bibliography is used to list all the sources used in preparing a paper. Many of these sources may already have appeared in the footnotes. Information given in bibliographic entries is generally the same as that in the footnotes and is presented in the same order. (See also *Footnotes, page 54*.) The style of presentation differs in the following ways:

- The author's *last* name is given first, followed by a comma, the author's *first name*, and then a period.

- The title is followed by a *period*.

- Page numbers are given *only* for a selection in an anthology or collection.

- *Each line* of an entry is *indented except the first*, so that the author's name is prominent.

- The entries are listed *alphabetically* by authors' last names.

- The list is not numbered.

Here is a standard entry in a bibliography:

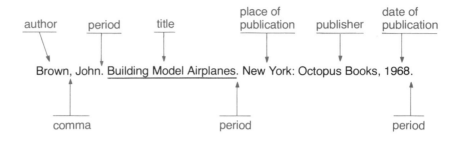

Brown, John. Building Model Airplanes. New York: Octopus Books, 1968.

If more than one place of publication is given, use the first place listed in the entry or the place closest to your home. The place closest to your home is probably where the book you used was actually published.

If more than one publication date is given, select the most recent date. If no date is given, simply put "n.d.", meaning "no date".

The bibliography is placed at the end of the research paper.

Like footnotes, bibliographic entries vary slightly according to the source being listed. Here are some examples of bibliographic entries:

- A book with one author or editor

  Jennings, Gary. Black Magic, White Magic. New York: Dial, 1964.

  Lang, Andrew, ed. Nursery Rhyme Book. London: Frederick Warne, 1965.

- A book with two authors or editors

  Boggs, Ralph Steele, and Mary Goule Davis. Three Golden Oranges and Other Spanish Folk Tales. New York: David McKay, 1964.

- A book with three or more authors or editors

  Bennett, Allan, *et al*. Electrons on the Move. New York: Walker, 1964.

- A work in a collection by several authors, with an editor

  Service, Robert. "The Cremation of Sam McGee." In Canadian Literature: The Beginnings to the 20th Century. Ed. Catherine M. McLay. Toronto: McClelland and Stewart Limited, 1974, pp. 412–15.

- A book that has been translated

  Dostoyevsky, Fyodor. Crime and Punishment. Trans. Sidney Monas. New York: The New American Library, 1968.

- An article with an author's name listed from a magazine, periodical, or encyclopedia

  Newman, Peter C. "What's So Surprising About Quebec's Anglo Exodus? They're Just Following Their Money." Maclean's, 4 April 1977, pp. 14–15.

  Scott, Peter. "Revolutionaries Pause for Breath." Times Educational Supplement, 23 June 1969, p. 21.

  Wolff, Eldon G. "Guns and Ammunition." New Book of Knowledge. New York: Grolier, 1968. 7:118–9.

Note: For multi-volume reference books, the volume and page numbers may be combined by using a colon. In the preceding example, the article "Guns and Ammunition" is in volume 7 on pages 118–9 of the *New Book of Knowledge*.

- A book or article with no author given

    "Elizabeth Murgatroyed 101 Years Old." Heritage, Sept.-Oct. 1975, pp. 20–1.

    "Seeds of Postal Strike Sown in 1966." Edmonton Journal, 7 August 1968, p. 10, col. 1–3.

    "Makerios III." Collier's Encyclopedia, 1968. 15:253.

- Pamphlets

    Smith, Bill R. "How We Spend Our Free Time." Public Affairs Pamphlet No. 23. Rev. ed. New York: Public Affairs Committee, 1973.

- Source sponsored by an institution, organization, society, or government department

    Favorite Folk Tales, Fairy Tales, and Legends Told Under the Green Umbrella. Association for Childhood Education International. New York: Macmillan, 1950.

Abbreviations Used in Footnotes and Bibliographies

anon.	=	anonymous
col.	=	column
cols.	=	columns
comp.	=	compiled
ed.	=	editor or edition
eds.	=	editors or editions
et al.	–	(Latin *et alii*) and others
Ibid.	=	(Latin *ibidem*) in the same place
n.d.	=	no date
p.	=	page
pp.	=	pages
rev.	=	revision or revised
rpt.	=	reprint
trans.	=	translated by
vol.	=	volume
vols.	=	volumes

Checklist for Bibliographies

Have I:

1. Indented the second and following lines of all entries?
2. Single-spaced all entries?
3. Double-spaced between all entries?
4. Listed all entries in alphabetical order?
5. Checked punctuation?

6. Reproduced all the necessary information in each entry *exactly* from the original source?

7. Placed the bibliography at the end of the paper on a separate page or pages?

Figures

Figures are maps, graphs, illustrations, tables, or diagrams used to convey information. These visual aids may be placed within the body of a research paper or on separate pages. Figures are not necessary or appropriate in *all* research papers.

If you think your paper will be enhanced by the inclusion of a figure, this is how to present one:

- Title the figure. Capitalize the first word only.
- Number the figure.
- Draw parallel lines to separate the title from the figure and the figure from the body of the paper.

Here is a figure, presented within the body of a paper:

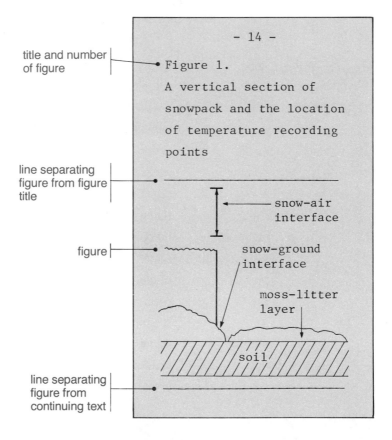

If a figure is not the product of your own mind, it must be footnoted. The footnote number is placed after the title.

All figures are listed on a separate sheet of paper following the Table of Contents. Figures are numbered in the order of their appearance, with the page numbers on which they can be found.

Graphs

The graph, which is a type of figure, is an effective way of presenting statistical data in a form that is quickly and easily understood. There are several types of graphs; which one you use depends upon the information you wish to convey. Each graph should have a title. The title and labels should be neatly hand-lettered. Coloured pencils are useful in identifying the various lines and sections, but they are not essential. If a paper has only one or two graphs, they should be listed in the Table of Figures. If there are three or more, a Table of Graphs should be included in the paper. A Table of Graphs follows the same format as a Table of Figures.

Examples of three common types of graphs are presented below.

1. Circle or Pie Graph

This is the simplest kind of graph. It is useful to express percentages. The angles at the centre should correspond to the percentages shown. (For example, the angle of the French section below should be 28.7% of 360°, or 103.3°.)

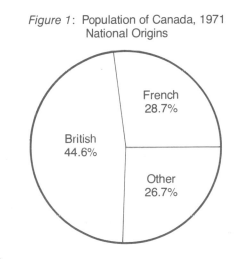

Figure 1: Population of Canada, 1971
National Origins

2. Line Graph

Line graphs are particularly useful to show trends.

Figure 2: Average Salaries of Professional Athletes

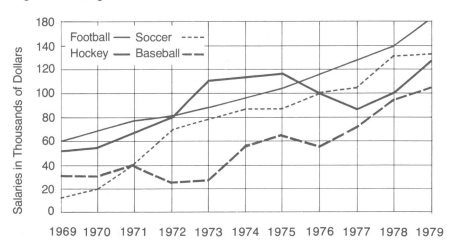

3. Bar Graph

Bar graphs may be used to make comparisons or to show trends.

Figure 3: Stopping Distances at Different Speeds for Automobiles

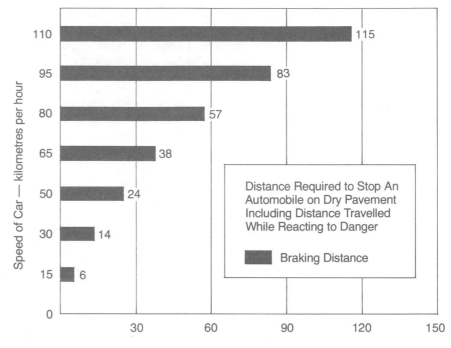

Appendix | An appendix contains material that supplements or expands upon topics in the main text. Most appendices are found in books or long scholarly papers, not in school research assignments. However, if an appendix is needed, it is placed ahead of the Footnotes page at the back of the paper.

If there is more than one appendix, a Table of Appendices is given at the front of the paper as well. This table should follow the same format as a Table of Contents. (See *page 54*).

REPORTS | You will not always be asked to prepare a piece of writing as detailed as a research paper. Instead, your teacher might ask you to write a *report*. A report is a written, systematic statement of facts prepared for a specific purpose and aimed at a specific reader. It is intended to inform or to explain.

A report differs from a research paper in several ways:

- It is usually shorter than a research paper.
- It usually involves less investigation of sources.
- It usually supplies less documentation; often it does not have footnotes.
- Details of sources usually appear in the text of the work.

Even though a report may differ from a research paper, you should expect to go through a similar process in preparing for and writing the report.

- Decide upon a topic.
- Search library research material.
- Prepare a preliminary bibliography.
- Limit the topic.
- Return to library resource material for more detailed information and note-taking.
- Record data from experiments or observations you make, if this is appropriate to the topic.
- Prepare a detailed outline of the topic.
- Write a rough draft.
- Reread and revise your work.
- Make a final copy and reread it before handing it in.

Because a report is designed to be a precise review of facts, it cannot contain everything that you know about a topic. However, collect as much material as you can. It is better to have too much information available rather than too little.

A report should give information to the reader in a clear and objective form. Each paragraph should begin with a topic sentence which makes clear what the paragraph will be about.

The information in a report should be factual, based on evidence from written or spoken sources or from the writer's observations.

SCIENTIFIC PAPERS

Scientific papers are research papers that are based on *experimentation and data collection*. They differ from other research papers in that the footnote references in a scientific paper are presented in a slightly different form. Also, a scientific paper has several parts not found in other papers. If you are writing a *formal laboratory report*, you should consult your teacher as to what format he or she would like you to follow.

Footnote References

In scientific papers, footnote references are written in abbreviated style and placed in parentheses *immediately after* the material for which credit is being given. These are called "embedded footnotes". This is how they are prepared:

- The writer's last name is followed by the date of publication. For example, (Smith 1977). No comma is needed.
- If there are two writers, both names are given. For example, (Smith and Jones 1973).
- When there are more than two writers, the name of the first writer is given followed by *et al*. For example, (Brown *et al*. 1980).

A list of *References* or *Works Cited* is placed on a separate page at the end of the paper, using the same format as a bibliography. (See *Bibliography, page 57*).

Sections Following is a sample table of contents from a scientific paper. It shows the various sections that such a paper may contain.

includes thesis statement

use subheadings where appropriate

if applicable, location where study was done

techniques and materials used

presentation of data, often using figures

account for results and their relationship to accepted scientific ideas

brief discussion of all material in point form

```
                Table of Contents
Table of Figures
Introduction                              1
  Background to the Problem               1
  Purpose of the Study                    4
The Study Area                            7
Methods                                  13
Results                                  19
Discussion                               27
Summary                                  36
References                               37
Appendices
A. (must have a title)                   40
B. ("        "    "    " )               42
C. ("        "    "    " )               43
Bibliography                             44
```

As a general guideline:

- Neatness always counts when presenting written work.

- Most "special" formats are designed to give information — like your name, the assignment number, or the name of a book you have quoted — in the clearest possible form.

- The rules for research papers can be looked up and followed carefully when you are asked to do a research paper.

Test Yourself:

1. What is missing from this essay title page?

   > The Politics of
   > Body-checking in Hockey

2. Although you need not try to memorize all the possible footnote formats, you should memorize the six things that you need to take down about a book you are using for a research paper. What are they?

3. Which style of graph would you choose to present the following types of information? Why?

   a) Comparing percentages of people speaking the five major languages in Canada

   b) Showing rate of inflation from 1945 to the present

CHAPTER 5
Checking Written Work

CHECKING WRITTEN WORK

Nothing a person writes the first time is perfect. Every writer needs to reread and revise. Use this Chapter to help polish your work -- to improve sentences, word usage, spelling, grammar, and punctuation. (The Index at the back of the book will also help you find what you need.)

CONTENTS

SENTENCES A good sentence clearly expresses the writer's ideas. There is one effective test for deciding whether or not a sentence is clear and complete. Ask: "Does it make sense?" The following are some common errors made in constructing sentences, along with suggestions to make sentences clear and effective.

Sentence Fragments

A fragment is a part of a sentence, punctuated as if the words formed a complete sentence. It can be confusing to the reader.

Avoid: Took off from Dominion Park in Montreal in July, 1906.

Acceptable: "The Flying Sausage", the first power-driven lighter-than-air craft to be flown in Canada, took off from Dominion Park in Montreal in July, 1906.

Avoid: When you walk into a darkened movie theatre.

Acceptable: When you walk into a darkened movie theatre, you often have to wait several seconds for your eyes to adjust to the dim light.

Note: Writers sometimes use sentence fragments for effect in fiction or magazine articles. However, fragments are inappropriate in formal pieces of writing such as essays and research papers.

As a general guideline:

- Make sure every sentence includes a subject and a verb and that it expresses a complete thought.

Test yourself:

1. Which of the following are sentence fragments?

   a) Easily scramble to the tops of tall trees.

   b) The lion, equipped with sharp teeth and powerful jaws, not lightly called the king of the jungle.

   c) The Siberian tiger, with a mass of up to 290 kg and measuring 4 m in length, surpasses any lion in size.

   d) Unlike lions and tigers, leopards inclined to attack humans if they are frightened.

   e) Although jaguars are carnivores, or meat eaters, many people are surprised to find that, in addition to small mammals, also have been known to catch and eat small fish.

2. Revise the sentences that you have identified as fragments so that they make complete sentences. There may be more than one way to revise any of the fragments.

Run-on Sentences

A run-on sentence is made up of two or more complete thoughts joined together by only a comma or simply written as one sentence, with no punctuation at all.

Avoid: The leaves are falling off the trees it will soon be winter.

Acceptable: The leaves are falling off the trees; it will soon be winter.

Avoid: We couldn't agree on how many cards to deal to each player, everyone had a different idea, Jake finally got out the rule book.

Acceptable: We couldn't agree on how many cards to deal to each player. Everyone had a different idea, so Jake finally got out the rule book.

As a general guideline:

- Use the correct punctuation for joining two complete thoughts: a comma plus a conjunction, or a semicolon. Do not join two complete thoughts with only a comma.

Test yourself:

1. Which of the following are run-on sentences?

    a) Hockey originated in Canada in the 1870s it quickly spread to the United States.

    b) Amateur hockey is popular worldwide and has been in the winter Olympic games since 1920.

    c) The Stanley Cup was first awarded in 1893 for the Canadian amateur championship, from 1912 to 1925 it was awarded to the winner of a competition between the champions of the Pacific Coast League and the Eastern League.

    d) Modern-day competition for the Stanley Cup occurs in the spring of each year between the best teams of the NHL in a succession of games called the playoffs, interestingly, these games are the only ones in which overtime periods are used to break ties.

2. Revise the sentences that you have identified as run-on sentences in question 1 so that they no longer run on. There are several ways to revise them.

Modifier Mistakes

A modifier is a word or phrase that describes another word or phrase in a sentence. When a modifier in a sentence is misplaced, the reader becomes confused.

1. **Misplaced Modifiers**
    Modifiers should be placed near the word they describe. Here are some examples of misplaced modifiers. The arrows show how to correct the sentences.

    A policeman clocked the dragster racing down the street in plain clothes.

    The prime minister was elected to barely a five-year term.

    Only Atlantic salmon can be caught in the early summertime.

    My sister laughed so hard that she cried almost.

As a general guideline:

- Decide what the modifying phrase or word logically refers to and place the modifier next to it.

Test yourself:

Several of the following sentences have misplaced modifiers. Identify the misplaced words or phrases, then decide where they should be placed in order for the sentence to make sense.

1. One of the most popular spy novel heroes of all time, James Bond, who wrote the Bond novels in the 1950s and early 1960s, was created by a British author named Ian Fleming.
2. Full of sex and violence, many parents tried to keep their teenage children from reading Ian Fleming's James Bond novels.
3. However, by today's standards, most of the material in Fleming's books is less violent than the evening news.
4. Although Ian Fleming died in 1964, Hollywood, apparently leaving Bond without a "father", has kept the Bond character alive with such movies as *From Russia With Love* and *Goldfinger*.

---

2. **Dangling Modifiers**

   A dangling modifier is a descriptive word or phrase that does not refer to anything in the sentence. It confuses the reader.

Avoid:	*Speeding across the goal line*, the coach jumped up from the bench and began to cheer.
Acceptable:	As the receiver sped across the goal line, the coach jumped up from the bench and began to cheer.
Avoid:	*Instead of studying*, the television was turned on.
Acceptable:	Instead of studying, I turned on the television.
Avoid:	*Producing 160 a minute*, Dennis Chinfen of Ottawa invented an automatic egg roll maker.
Acceptable:	An automatic egg roll maker, invented by Dennis Chinfen of Ottawa, produces 160 egg rolls a minute.

As a general guideline:

- Decide what the modifier refers to and *insert* that word or phrase in the sentence.

Test yourself:

Several of the following sentences contain dangling modifiers. Identify them, then revise the sentences so that they make sense. There are several ways to revise any of the sentences that contain dangling modifiers.

1. Always quick to see through a Spectre plot, the high style of James Bond's life did not appear to interfere with business.

2. Beautiful women, fast cars, and unusual talents were the tricks of Bond's trade.

3. Relying on his skill in oriental martial arts, most enemy agents were instantly defeated.

4. Activating the special rocket engines, the sports car sped out ahead in every car chase.

Awkward Sentences

There are many kinds of awkward sentences. Often, the information in them does not follow a logical sequence.

Avoid: Mario and I, after trying to solve the equation for about two hours, because we were ready to give up, consulted the physics teacher.

Acceptable: After trying for about two hours to solve the equation, Mario and I were ready to give up, so we consulted the physics teacher.

As a general guideline:

- Think carefully about how the various parts of the sentence relate to one another.
- Decide on the best system for arranging the parts — for example, according to time or order of importance — and then follow that system.

Test yourself:

Here are three awkward sentences. Rearrange the words so that the sentences read smoothly.

1. The party in power, after several scandals, called an election, bitterly criticized by the opposition.
2. As the worst of the scandals concerned oil price negotiations, the opposition, a subject of considerable interest to the public, had the support of the people.
3. Increasingly, resources are, whether oil, water, or mineral, high-powered issues in the political arena.

Parallelism

The clearest way to list similar items or events in a series is to make them match one another in form. This is called parallelism.

Avoid: Massive pyramids, the carefully controlled and intricate writing used in hieroglyphics, and eerie mummies come to mind when I think of ancient Egypt.

Acceptable: Massive pyramids, intricate hieroglyphics, and eerie mummies come to mind when I think of ancient Egypt.
(Each item in the list is now in the same form.)

As a general guideline:

• Identify the items you wish to list and put each in the same form.

Test yourself:

Each of the following sentences contains at least one error in parallelism. Revise the sentences so that they follow the principle of parallelism. Leave out any words that are unnecessary when the parts of each sentence are placed in parallel form.

1. Thebes, Memphis, Alexandria, which is located on the northern coast of Africa, and Gizeh were all important cities in ancient Egypt.

2. The Mediterranean Sea, the Red Sea of biblical fame, the life-giving Nile, and Lake Nasser are all bodies of water that are important to the economy of modern-day Egypt.

Subject-Verb Agreement

Every sentence must have a subject and a verb. The subject and verb must match (or agree) in number. The word in the sentence that decides number is the subject. A singular subject must take a singular verb form; a plural subject must take a plural verb form.

Avoid: *Drought*, followed by food shortages, remain a serious threat to the stability of the poor nations of the world.

Acceptable: *Drought*, followed by food shortages, remains a serious threat to the stability of the poor nations of the world

In some cases, you may not be sure whether the subject of a sentence is singular or plural. The following are some situations which may create difficulty.

1. **Plural-Sounding Endings**
   Many nouns have a plural-sounding ending but are actually singular in meaning. Some examples are *news*, *mumps*, *measles*, and *economics*.

   > *Economics* in the twentieth century *has been* dominated by the theories of John Maynard Keynes.

2. **Compound Subjects**
   Two or more singular nouns, joined together by the word *and* and functioning as the compound subject of a sentence, require a plural verb.

   > Her *mittens*, *scarf*, *and ears were* a beautiful shade of blue on that cold morning.

3. **Collective Nouns**
   Collective nouns usually require a *singular* verb. Some common collective nouns are *group, army, crowd, bunch*, and *family*.

   > *The French army* that gathered on the Plains of Abraham *was* under the leadership of General Louis Montcalm.

4. **"Either . . . or" and Similar Word Pairs**
   When a compound subject is linked by words such as *either . . . or*, *neither . . . nor*, *not only . . . but also*, and *whether . . . or*, the part of the subject nearest the verb determines whether the verb is singular or plural.

   > Neither the teacher nor *the students were* able to answer the question raised by the visiting lecturer.

   > Whether the trees or *the wind was* responsible we'll never know.

5. **Indefinite Pronouns**
   Indefinite pronouns ending in *-one*, *-body*, and *-thing* always require a singular verb. Here is a list of some of these pronouns:

anyone	anybody	anything
everyone	everybody	everything
no one	nobody	nothing
someone	somebody	something

   Everyone is here now.

   No one really *understands* how the universe began.

   Something is coming out of the shadows!

6. **Quantities**
   A subject naming a quantity usually requires a singular verb. This rule applies to quantities of *time, money, distance*, and *weight*.

   > *Ten minutes is* a long time when you're waiting for the next UFO.

   > *Thirty dollars is* the approximate cost of a dozen roses.

7. **Pronouns that Vary in Being Singular or Plural**
   The following are some pronouns that are either singular or plural, depending on their use in a specific sentence: *some, all, none, more, most, any, such*.

   > *All* of the *apple is* gone.

   > *All* of the *apples are* gone.

As a general guideline:

- Identify the true subject of the sentence.
- Match the verb to the subject.
- Consult the above list of special situations whenever you are in doubt.

Test yourself:

The following sentences contain errors in subject-verb agreement. Identify them and supply the correct words.

1. Tradition has it that the heart, shaped in our mind's eye like the decoration on a Valentine's card, control our emotions.

2. Most people, however, now realizes that all thought, whether emotional or rational, originate in the brain.

3. Occasionally, the evening news carry a story on a recent discovery about the brain, but we all remains largely ignorant of the recent exciting advances in brain research.

4. When you consider that around three dollars buy a good basic paperback on the brain, why do anyone remain confused about the workings of the brain?

Verb Tense

The tense of a verb indicates time, that is, past, present, or future. Here are some guidelines for choosing the correct verb tense:

1. **Mixed Tenses**

   The tense of all verbs should usually be the same within a sentence or throughout a piece of writing. Mix verb tenses *only* when the thoughts you are expressing require it.

   Avoid: The stadium *was* filled to capacity, and people *are* even standing in the aisles.

   Acceptable: The stadium *was* filled to capacity, and people *were* even standing in the aisles.

   Acceptable: Although Newfoundland *is* sparsely populated today, we *will* doubtless *see* an increase in its population as a consequence of the recent natural resources discoveries.

2. **Participles**

   When the verb you choose contains a participle, include an auxiliary (or helping) verb to complete the verb.

   a) Present participles end in *-ing*. When they are used, add a form of the verb *to be* to complete the verb.

      Not Acceptable: I *talking*.
      He *running*.

      Acceptable: I *am talking*.
      He *was running*.

   b) Past participles, if they are different from the simple past forms of the verbs, require the addition of a form of the verb *to have*. Some examples are *chosen*, *driven*, and *done*.

      Not Acceptable: He *driven* a car.
      We *done* many things.

Acceptable: He *has driven* a car.
We *have done* many things.

3. **Past Perfect, Present Perfect, and Future Perfect**
   To distinguish between two events that happened in the past and to show that one event took place before the other, use the past perfect tense.

   Past perfect = *had* + past participle

   By the time her plane *took off* (past), I *had* already *driven* (past perfect) home from the airport.

   To distinguish between two events occurring at two different times in the present, use the present perfect tense.

   Present perfect = *have* (or *has*) + past participle

   Cheryl *has left* (present perfect) the house and *is waiting* (present) at the corner for a bus.

   To distinguish between two events occurring at two different times in the future, use the future perfect tense.

   Future perfect = *will* + *have* + past participle

   I *will call* (future) him tomorrow at six, because by that time I *will have decided* (future perfect) what to ask him.

As a general guideline:

- Distinguish carefully between past, present, future, past perfect, present perfect, and future perfect.
- Make the verb you choose express your thought.
- Consult the list of irregular verbs on page 91 if you are in doubt about any forms.

Test yourself:

Each of the following sections contains an error in verb tense. Name the error, then correct it.

1. I need to go on a diet because my pants were too tight.

2. Exercise is supposed to help you lose weight, so I jogging every morning before school now.

3. Yesterday, my mother wanted to jog with me, but by the time she mentioned it, I already jogged two kilometres.

Using Pronouns

A pronoun is a word that takes the place of a noun or another pronoun. Choose a pronoun that matches (or agrees) with the word it has replaced.

1. Kinds of Pronouns

a) *Personal pronouns* are often classified into the nominative or objective form. The *nominative* form of a personal pronoun is used when the pronoun is the subject of a verb or when the pronoun follows a form of the verb *to be*. The *objective* form of a personal pronoun is used when the pronoun is the object of a verb or when the pronoun follows a preposition. Here is a list of the personal pronouns:

Singular	Nominative	Objective
1st person	I	me
2nd person	you	you
3rd person	he, she, it	him, her, it

Plural		
1st person	we	us
2nd person	you	you
3rd person	they	them

Here is how the above chart can be applied:

Avoid: *Joe and me* are interested in the game.

Acceptable: *Joe and I* are interested in the game.

Avoid: There are never any secrets between *she and I*.

Acceptable: There are never any secrets between *her and me*.

Avoid: It was *her* who designed the cover.

Acceptable: It was *she* who designed the cover.

b) A *relative pronoun* is a pronoun that introduces a dependent clause in a sentence and refers to a word or a group of words in the main clause. There are four *relative pronouns*:

- *That* and *which* refer to everything except people.
- *Who* and *whom* refer to people.

   Who is the nominative form (of the pronoun).

   Whom is the objective form (of the pronoun).

The arrows below indicate the words to which the various pronouns refer:

Here is the way that the table should be set.

Zucchini, which I detest, grows especially well in our garden.

Our next-door neighbour, who was born in Munich, makes an excellent dish called sauerbrauten.

Mac, whom I met five years ago, is nearly two metres tall.

c) An *indefinite pronoun* is a pronoun that does not specify the identity of what it refers to (or describes). Some *indefinite pronouns* may give you trouble.

-one, -body, -thing
Pronouns ending in *-one*, *-body*, or *-thing* (as well as the pronoun *one*) require a singular verb.

Avoid:	*Everyone* is doing *their* best.
Acceptable:	*Everyone* is doing *her* (or *his*) best.
Avoid:	*Nobody* wore *their* sweaters.
Acceptable:	*Nobody* wore *his* (or *her*) sweater.
Avoid:	*One* should be attentive to the complaints of *your* body when jogging.
Acceptable:	*One* should be attentive to the complaints of *her* (or *his*) body when jogging.

Note: If you are uncomfortable using a masculine or feminine pronoun to refer to both sexes, you can often rewrite the sentence. For example:

All people should do *their* best.

One should be attentive to the complaints of *one's* body when jogging.

The pronouns *all*, *none*, and *some* may be singular or plural in meaning.

All (meaning *everything*) *was* peaceful and quiet in the early morning.

All (*of the people*) *were* in their seats.

None (*of the boys*) *practise* more regularly than Tim.

None (*of the cake*) *was* left.

Some (of the apples) *are* red and *some* (of the apples) *are* green.

Some (of the water) *flows* through the cracks in the pipe and *is* wasted.

2. **Pronoun Reference**
Be sure that the reader can easily identify the pronoun's antecedent (the word or words the pronoun has replaced).

Avoid:	I followed the recipe to the letter, but *they* don't seem to make a cake.
Acceptable:	I followed the recipe to the letter, but *the ingredients* don't seem to make a cake. *They* make a cracker.
Avoid:	Tim didn't write any letters to Phil when *he* was at camp.
Acceptable:	When *Tim* was at camp, *he* didn't write any letters to Phil.

As a general guideline:

- Make personal pronouns agree in person, number, and form.
- Make relative pronouns agree with either people (*who, whom*) or things (*that, which*).
- Replace indefinite pronouns such as *anyone, somebody,* or *anything* only with some form of *he, she,* or *it.*
- Make sure that the pronoun has an antecedent within the sentence or in the preceding sentence.
- Make sure that there is only one possible antecedent.

Test yourself:

1. Which pronouns in the following sentences have been used incorrectly? Why? Check your answers before going on to question 2.

   a) Charles Panati, in their book entitled *Breakthroughs*, reports some exciting discoveries in the prevention of tooth decay.

   b) Decay commonly attacks the teeth in our mouths, and they are eventually painful.

   c) Fortunately, the problem of tooth decay, who affects millions of people each year, may soon be a thing of the past.

   d) Wouldn't it be wonderful, though, if everyone could eat as much candy as they wanted?

2. In the sentences above, replace the incorrectly used pronouns with the correct choices. In some cases, you may have to change the sentence slightly.

Adverb Errors

Adverbs are used to modify verbs, adjectives, and other adverbs. Most adjectives can be made into adverbs simply by adding *-ly*. For example, *slow* (adjective) becomes *slowly* (adverb). Avoid confusing adverbs with adjectives.

Avoid: He did *real* well on the exam.

Acceptable: He did *really* well on the exam.

Avoid: The golfer played that shot *perfect*.

Acceptable: The golfer played that shot *perfectly*.

As a general guideline:

- Remember that adverbs modify verbs, adjectives, and other adverbs. Adjectives modify *only* nouns and pronouns.

Test yourself:

Insert words that make sense and are grammatically correct. All of your answers will be either adverbs or adjectives.

1. Desserts made using maple sugar or syrup are _____ sweet.

2. Both these sweet substances are produced by a _____ process that involves "tapping" sugar or black maple trees.

3. The Indians were the first to take advantage of the _____ special properties of maple trees.

4. Later, colonists in Quebec and Vermont _____ followed the Indians' _____ example every spring.

Conjunctions ("Joining" Words)

Conjunctions are words that join other words or groups of words.

And and *but* are one type of conjunction. *And* is used to link two similar thoughts; *but* is used to link two contrasting thoughts.

Avoid: Italy can trace its history back to the year 753 B.C., *and* the United States can only trace back to the year 1620 A.D.

Acceptable: Italy can trace its history back to the year 753 B.C., *but* the United States can only trace back to the year 1620 A.D.

Another type of conjunction is used to link two parallel parts in a sentence. This conjunction is always used in pairs.

neither . . . nor	both . . . and	
either . . . or	not only . . . but also	
whether . . . or		

Each of these pairs has a specific meaning. You cannot mix the pairs. For example, *neither* always comes with *nor*; *both* always comes with *and*.

Avoid: *Both* West Germany *and also* Japan have developed powerful postwar economies.

Acceptable: *Both* West Germany *and* Japan have developed powerful postwar economies.

As a general guideline:

• Think carefully about what you are trying to say and choose a link that is appropriate to your thought.

Test yourself:

Insert pairs of conjunctions that make sense and are grammatically correct.

1. _____ the French-speaking people of Quebec are called Quebecois _____ "francophones", it is an undeniable fact that they have been in Canada for hundreds of years.

2. Some might say that the Quebecois are _____ French _____ Canadian, but something altogether unique.

3. Nevertheless, _____ Canada as a whole _____ Quebec as a province must come to some resolution of where the Quebecois stand in national terms.

4. Obviously, this resolution will only be possible if _____ English _____ French-speaking Canadians are willing to talk constructively.

Double Negatives

A double negative — that is, the use of two negative words to express one negative thought — can confuse the reader. If you mean to say something negative and put *two* negatives in a sentence, you actually create a positive.

Avoid: Julius Caesar did *not* have *no* idea that the senators were conspiring to assassinate him.

Acceptable: Julius Caesar did *not* have *any* idea that the senators were conspiring to assassinate him.

Acceptable: Julius Caesar had *no* idea that the senators were conspiring to assassinate him.

Avoid: Janet decided to try out for the team *irregardless* of the fact that she wouldn't be sixteen until December.

Acceptable: Janet decided to try out for the team *regardless* of the fact that she wouldn't be sixteen until December.

The words *barely, hardly,* and *scarcely* are negative in meaning; therefore, do not combine any of these words with a negative such as *not*.

Avoid: Louis Pasteur *didn't hardly* establish a good working relationship with his colleagues.

Acceptable: Louis Pasteur *hardly* established a good working relationship with his colleagues.

As a general guideline:

- Use only one negative word or word part to negate one idea.
- Never use a negative word with *barely*, *hardly*, or *scarcely*.

Test yourself:

Identify the double negatives in the sentences below, then revise them so that they are not confusing. There is more than one way to revise any of the sentences. Try to choose the way that makes the most sense.

1. We haven't never found out the actual date of the first Olympic games, but tradition places the date at 776 B.C.
2. The Greeks hardly never forgot that Zeus was the god in whose honour the games were held.
3. Today, however, no one barely remembers that the Olympics began as a religious festival.

Redundancy and Repetition

When more than one word or phrase in a sentence expresses the same idea, the result is a weak sentence. The error is called *redundancy*. For example:

- repeat *again*
- *true* fact
- *very* unique
- *new* innovation
- *old* adage

Watch for sentences like this in your writing:

Weak: *In my opinion, I think* that *unmarried bachelors* should be encouraged to marry.

Acceptable: *I think bachelors* should be encouraged to marry.

Acceptable: *Bachelors* should be encouraged to marry.

Repetition of the same word several times in a sentence or paragraph tends to bore the reader. Try to find alternative ways to express ideas. For example, you might decide to use a pronoun in place of a noun or to reword a sentence. Be as concise as possible. (See also *Variety, page 34*.)

Avoid: The *coach attempted* to find a suitable *replacement* for the *quarterback*, but the *attempt* failed; finally the *coach* had to *replace* the *quarterback* with a rookie.

Acceptable: The coach attempted but failed to find a suitable replacement for the quarterback; he finally had to send in a rookie.

As a general guideline:

• Ask yourself, "Could any of the words in this sentence be removed without changing the meaning of the sentence?" If the answer is yes, begin removing words.

• Try not to use the same word several times in a sentence; vary the words you use.

• Express your ideas concisely.

Test yourself:

The following sentences are redundant and repetitious. What words can you remove or change to improve these sentences?

1. The well-known and famous Canadian author, Stephen Leacock, once wrote a paper discussing the question of whether the bicycle or the horse is the nobler creature.

2. Leacock points out that the horse is covered, from head to toe, with hair.

3. On the other hand, he continues, the bicycle is not completely covered with hair, except for the 1889 model of the bicycle that a great many people are riding in the American state of Idaho.

4. The author concludes by finishing with the statement that he now understands why horsemen spend so little time sitting down when they are not on their gallant steeds or mounts.

Mixed Metaphors   A *mixed metaphor* occurs when the writer loses sight of the point of comparison between two objects and makes illogical connections between them. A mixed metaphor weakens the image and may confuse the reader. (See also *Figurative Language, page 35*.)

The Grand Canyon of Jane's depression reached its height when she failed her swimming test.

The first image makes a connection between Jane's depression and the depth and vastness of the Grand Canyon. But the comparison becomes silly when the idea of height is added to the metaphor. Often a statement of simple fact is better than a confusing metaphor.

As a general guideline:

- Decide what you are comparing to what and use only words that relate to that comparison.

Test yourself:

Here are three sentences containing mixed metaphors. Revise the sentences so that they make sense.

1. Don has been losing weight by leaps and bounds.
2. Mentally taking pen in hand, I sat down to type a letter to the employment office.
3. As we embark on the road of life, we should remember not to throw a monkey wrench into our goals.

Tone and Sentence Type

There are four types of sentence: *statement, exclamation, question,* and *command*. Each type says something distinctive about the writer's point of view. Each conveys a different tone.

Consider the following four sentences. Notice how dramatically the sentence type changes the writer's tone.

Statement:	A better gymnasium is definitely needed for sporting events. (Writer sees no room for argument.)
Exclamation:	What an improvement it would be to have a better gymnasium for sporting events! (Writer is thoroughly convinced, an enthusiastic supporter of the change.)
Question:	Do we need a better gymnasium for sporting events? (Writer may be undecided.)
Command:	Help us to find a way to build a better gymnasium for sporting events. (Writer is convinced and seeking the support of others.)

As a general guideline:

- Think about the tone you want to convey and choose the sentence type that best expresses this tone.

Test yourself:

Here are four unpunctuated sentences. Identify the sentence type and add the correct punctuation.

1. Too few people take seriously their right to vote

2. Don't take your right to vote lightly

3. Do people take the right to vote seriously

4. People ought to take the right to vote seriously

Word Order and Ideas

The *arrangement* of the words and phrases you choose to present information will have a significant influence on the *idea* that you convey. Note how the *emphasis* in the following three sentences, all about the same topic, changes according to the arrangement of the words.

> The Canadian Shield, which covers more than half of Canada, *was the first part of North America to be permanently elevated above sea level*, and yet, even today, it remains largely undeveloped.

> *The first part of North America to be permanently elevated above sea level was the Canadian Shield*, a land mass that remains largely undeveloped today and occupies more than half of Canada.

> Largely undeveloped today, the Canadian Shield, covering more than half of Canada, *was the first part of North America to be permanently elevated above sea level*.

As a general guideline:

- Carefully reread each sentence you have written.
- Identify what you wish to have stand out as the main idea of the sentence. In sentences where your central point does not stand out, rearrange the words and phrases to emphasize the main idea.

Test yourself:

Here are three good sentences. Imagine that you would like to change the emphasis in each of them so as to highlight the underlined words. How would you do it?

1. In a disaster, the availability of heat, light, shelter, food, and water becomes *critically important*.

2. People who know first aid are indispensable in any kind of disaster *because regular medical personnel are rarely able to keep up with the increased demand for services*.

3. Although most of us are inclined to think of *food and water* as the primary necessities of life, one winter night spent in the open air without heat or light would probably cause us to reorder our priorities.

USING THE DICTIONARY

The sample dictionary entries below illustrate some of the ways in which a dictionary can be useful to you.*

plenty ⎯⎯ guide words (first and
plover ⎯⎯ last entries on a page)

pronunciation key ⎯⎯⎯⎯⎯→

hat, āge, cãre, fär; let, ēqual, tėrm; it, Īce
hot, ōpen, ôrder; oil, out; cup, pùt, rüle, ūse
əbove, takən, pencəl, lemən, circəs
ch, child; ng, long; sh, ship
th, thin; ŦH, then; zh, measure

irregular forms of
verbs ⎯⎯⎯⎯→

plot (plot) *n. v.* **plot·ted, plot·ting.** —*n.* **1** a secret plan, especially to do something wrong: *Two men formed a plot to rob the bank.* **2** the plan or main story of a play, novel, poem, etc. **3** a small piece of ground: *a garden plot.* **4** a map; diagram.

4 meanings as noun ⎯⎯⎯→

—*v.* **1** plan secretly with others; plan. **2** divide (land) into plots. **3** make a map or diagram of. **4** mark the position of (something) on a map or diagram: *The admiral plotted the position of all the ships in the fleet.* **5** in mathematics: **a** determine the location of a point by means of its co-ordinates; mark a point on graph paper. **b** make a curve by connecting points marked out on a graph. **c** represent (an equation, etc.) by means of a curve drawn through points on a graph. [OE *plot* patch of ground; meaning influenced by *complot* a joint plot (< F)] —**plot′less,** *adj.* —**plot′ter,** *n.*

5 meanings as verb ⎯⎯⎯→

word origin ⎯⎯⎯→

derivations ⎯⎯⎯→

Syn. *n.* **1** intrigue, conspiracy. –*v.* **1** Plot, conspire, scheme = plan secretly. **Plot** = form secretly, alone or together with others, a carefully designed plan, usually harmful or treacherous, against a person, group, or country: *Enemy agents plotted to blow up the plant.* **Conspire** emphasizes the combining of one person or group with another, usually secretly, to carry out an illegal act, especially treachery or treason: *They conspired to overthrow the government.* **Scheme** suggests careful planning, often in a crafty or underhand way, to gain one's own ends: *He schemed to become president.*

synonyms and usage ⎯⎯→

plough or **plow** (plou) *n.* **1** a big, heavy farm implement for cutting the soil and turning it over. **2** a machine for removing snow; snowplough.
—*v.* **1** turn over (soil) with a plough. **2** use a plough. **3** move as a plough does; advance slowly and with effort. **4** remove with a plough or as if with a plough: *plough up old roots.* **5** furrow: *plough a field, wrinkles ploughed in one's face by time.* **6** cut the surface of (water). **7** *Esp.Brit. Informal.* reject (a candidate) or be rejected in an examination. **8** plough back, reinvest (profits) in the same business. **9** plough into, *Informal.* **a** hit hard or at speed and travel into: *The car went out of control and ploughed into the building.* **b** undertake (a job, project, etc.) with energy and determination. **10** plough under, **a** plough into the ground to make manure. **b** defeat; destroy; overwhelm. [OE *plōg*] —**plough′er** or **plow′er,** *n.*

alternative spellings ⎯⎯→

idioms ⎯⎯⎯→

entry word showing syllables ⎯⎯⎯→

plough·boy or **plow·boy** (plou′boi′) *n.* **1** boy who guides the horses drawing a plough. **2** a country boy.

Here are some tips that will help you to use a dictionary efficiently.

1. **Meaning**

   Many words have more than one meaning or use. The first definition given is usually the most common.

2. **Spelling**

   Unfamiliar words will be easier to find if you can locate the first syllable or two. This search can be tricky, because words are not always spelled exactly as they sound. For example:

   • An *f*-sound may be spelled ph as in physician.

   • A *g*-sound may be spelled gh as in ghost or gu as in guest.

* From Canadian Senior Dictionary by Walter S. Avis et al
Copyright © Gage Publishing Limited 1979,
Reprinted by permission of Gage Publishing Limited

- A *j*-sound may be spelled g as in general.
- A *k*-sound may be spelled ch as in chord.
- A short *o*-sound may be spelled au as in August or aw as in awful.
- A *sh*-sound may be spelled ch as in chute, sch as in schism, ci as in social, ti as in motion, or just s as in sure.
- A *sk*-sound may be spelled sch as in scheme or sc as in scare.
- An *s*-sound may be spelled sc as in scene or ps as in psalm.
- A silent *k*, *g*, or *p* may occur before n as in know, gnaw, or pneumonia.
- A silent *w* may occur before r as in wrong.

3. **Syllabication**
Entry words of more than one syllable are often shown in syllables, so you can find the best place to make a break when you must divide a long word at the end of a line.

4. **Irregular Verb Forms**
Verb forms that change their spelling before *-ed* and *-ing*, such as *stir: stirred, stirring*, or verbs that change their form from tense to tense, such as *see: saw, seen, seeing*, are usually shown following the entry word.

5. **Pronunciation**
If you have seen a word written but are not sure how to pronounce it, check the phonetic version, usually given in parentheses after the entry word. Study the pronunciation key, given either on each page or at the beginning of the dictionary. Note the light (′) and heavy (′) stress marks.

6. **Word Origins (Etymology)**
The origin of each root word is often given after the definition. (An interpretation of the symbols is usually to be found at the front of the dictionary.) Often a glance at a word's origin will help make its meaning clear. For example, when you know that the word *distract* comes from the Latin word *tractus*, "draw", and the prefix *dis-*, "away", the meaning becomes clear.

7. **Synonyms and Usage**
Within a dictionary definition, or listed separately after the entry, there are often other words that mean the same or almost the same as the word you are looking up. Sometimes a special usage note is given, as in the illustration under the word *plot*. These notes will help you to choose *exactly* the right word for the idea you wish to convey.

As a general guideline:
- Consult the charts, "keys", and directions at the front of the dictionary whenever the meaning of a symbol is unclear.
- Take the time to read the entry carefully if you are looking for more than the correct spelling of the word you looked up.

SPELLING: SIX COMMON SPELLING QUESTIONS ANSWERED

There are few "rules" in spelling that do not have exceptions. The following guidelines can be useful, but when in doubt, always refer to a dictionary.

1. **How do I know if a word is spelled *ie* or *ei*?**

   Learn this saying:

   "Put I before E
   Except after C
   Or when sounded like A"

   field, thief, believe, chief, friend
   receive, ceiling, receipt, deceive
   neighbour, freight, eight, sleigh

   Note these exceptions:

   either, neither, height, seize, leisure, weird, science, protein

2. **How do I know when to drop the final -e if I am adding a suffix?**

   a) Drop the final -e when the suffix to be added begins with a vowel.

race + -ing	=	racing
love + -able	=	lovable
desire + -ous	=	desirous
structure + -al	=	structural
nonsense + -ical	=	nonsensical

   Note that words ending in -ce or -ge are exceptions:

face + -al	=	facial
province + -al	=	provincial
space + -ous	=	spacious
notice + -able	=	noticeable
manage + -able	=	manageable
courage + -ous	=	courageous

   b) Keep the final -e when the suffix to be added begins with a consonant.

sincere + -ly	=	sincerely
arrange + -ment	=	arrangement
shape + -less	=	shapeless
decisive + -ness	=	decisiveness
whole + -some	=	wholesome

   Note these exceptions:

argue + -ment	=	argument
due + -ly	=	duly
nine + -th	=	ninth
true + -ly	=	truly

3. **When do I double the final consonant if I am adding a suffix?**

   a) Never double the final consonant when the suffix to be added begins with a consonant.

commi*t* + -*m*ent = commi*t*ment
we*t* + -*n*ess = we*t*ness

b) Usually double the final consonant when the suffix to be added begins with a vowel.

commi*t* + -*i*ng = commi*tt*ing
prefe*r* + -ed = prefe*rr*ed
begi*n* + -*i*ng = begi*nn*ing
wi*n* + -er = wi*nn*er
ru*n* + -*i*ng = ru*nn*ing

Note these exceptions:
- If the accent is not on the last syllable, the final consonant is not doubled:

benefi*t* + -ed = benefi*t*ed
profi*t* + -ing = profi*t*ing
ope*n* + -ing = ope*n*ing

- Words ending in a single vowel and -*l* double the -*l* before a suffix that begins with a vowel.

leve*l* + -*i*ng = leve*ll*ing
trave*l* + -er = trave*ll*er

4. **When do I change the final -*y* to -*i* if I am adding a suffix?**

a) If the final -*y* follows a consonant, change the -*y* to -*i*.

melo*dy* + -ous = melo*di*ous
ba*by* + -s = ba*bi*es
hap*py* + -est = hap*pi*est
sil*ly* + -er = sil*li*er
mer*ry* + -ly = mer*ri*ly
plen*ty* + -ful = plen*ti*ful

Note these exceptions:

pi*ty* + -ous = pi*te*ous
plen*ty* + -ous = plen*te*ous

b) If the final -*y* follows a vowel, keep the -*y*.
pla*y* + -ed = pla*y*ed
donke*y* + -s = donke*y*s
jo*y* + -ful = jo*y*ful

Note these exceptions:
If the suffix -*ing* is to be added, always keep the -*y*.

pra*y* + -ing = pra*y*ing
tr*y* + -ing = tr*y*ing
marr*y* + -ing = marr*y*ing
to*y* + -ing = to*y*ing

5. **What do I do when I add the suffix -ly to a word ending in -l already?**

Make no change. Just add -ly.

wonderful + -ly	= wonderfully
casual + -ly	= casually
continual + -ly	= continually
official + -ly	= officially

6. **When do I double the s when adding dis- or mis- at the beginning of a word?**

Make no changes. Just add dis- or mis-.

| dis + -appear | = disappear |
| mis + -spell | = misspell |

There are no exceptions.

As a general guideline:

- Look carefully at new words as you find them in your reading, so you can form a clear mental image of them.
- Familiarize yourself with the rules and exceptions.
- Make your own list of problem words and study it often.
- Use a dictionary frequently.

Test yourself:

The following paragraph contains many common spelling errors. Correct them, reminding yourself of the rules and exceptions as you do so. Use a dictionary if you are uncertain.

> The role of the train in Canadian life has changed dramaticaly over the coarse of this century. Where once train travel was the most desireable mode of transportashun, today frieght, not passengers, keeps the cars runing on thier tracks. People who still chose train travel usualy recieve excellent service from personel, but no one denys that trains move slowlly as compared too airplanes. Some people beleive that there has been a noticable increase in train travel due to skyrocketing airfairs. Nevertheless, because people who travel most truely benefit from the speed of air travel, the skys are bound to become increasingly the prefered "travel ground".

HYPHENATED WORDS

Here is a chart of the most common types of hyphenated words:

Category	Key Words	Examples	Rule
Numbers	twenty-one	ninety-nine	Spelled-out, compound numbers between twenty-one and ninety-nine are hyphenated.
	one-half	three-fourths, two-fifths, seven-eighths	Spelled-out fractions require a hyphen between numerator and denominator.
	two-metre wall	1000-m race, five-litre can	When a number + a unit of measure precedes a noun, put a hyphen between the number and the unit.
	eight-year-old girl	seventy-year-old school, a two-year-old	When writing a number + *year* + *old*, put a hyphen after the number and after *year*.
	one-thirty	five-fifteen, eight-twenty	When spelling out time, put a hyphen between the hour and the minutes.
	twelve-odd occasions	150-odd books, thirty-odd participants	When writing a number + *odd*, separate the two with a hyphen.
Commonly Hyphenated Prefixes	pro-American	pre-Christian, all-Canadian	When placing a prefix before a proper name, separate the two with a hyphen.
	self-centred	self-control, self-*confident*	When combining *self* with another word, put a hyphen after *self*.
	all-seeing	all-powerful, all-knowing *but* all right, almost	When combining *all* + another word, put a hyphen after *all*.
	half-baked	half-life, half-mast *but* halfway	When combining *half* + another word, put a hyphen after *half*.
Family Relationships	sister-in-law	brothers-in-law, mother-in-law	When writing *in-law*, put a hyphen after the relationship word and after *in*.
	great-grandmother	great-aunt, great-great-grandfather	When writing of *great* family relationships, put a hyphen after each *great*.

Compound Modifiers Preceding the Word They Modify	thirst-quenching drink	Canadian-made piano, smoke-filled room, time-saving device	Hyphenate a combination of word + participle when the compound precedes a noun.
	well-known region	best-dressed entrant, ill-conceived plan, little-understood principle	Compound adjectives preceding a noun are hyphenated *unless* they are also modified.
		but very ill con-ceived plan	
Clarifying Hyphens	Re-cover the chair after you've recovered from the accident.	I re-created the garden for recreation.	Hyphenate prefixes when confusion with other words is possible.
Cases in which No Hyphen is Needed	quickly finished job	beautifully executed jump, terribly confused speech	Compound modifiers with adverbs ending in *-ly* are never hyphenated.
	prewar	pre-, post-, over-, under-, intra-, extra-, sub-, super-, pro-, anti-, co-, non-, un-, semi-, supra-	The prefixes in the adjoining column are never followed by a hyphen *except* when they are joined to a proper name.

As a general guideline:

- Consult a dictionary.
- Consult the chart in this section.

Test yourself:

Insert hyphens in the following paragraph where necessary.

> My ten year old sister was very proud to be a contestant in the city wide games. Her event was the hundred metre dash, and we all knew she would be up against terribly stiff competition. Although her starting time was eight fifteen in the morning, even our great grandmother came to watch. I think it made my sister a little self conscious to have our big family as a cheering section.

REGULAR AND IRREGULAR WORDS

Nouns

1. **How nouns change to form the plural**

   a) Most nouns add -*s* to form the plural.

Singular	Plural
chair	chairs
picture	pictures
ghost	ghosts

   b) When an extra syllable must be pronounced to make the -*s* sound clear, -*es* is added to form the plural.

Singular	Plural
church	churches
dish	dishes
dress	dresses
suffix	suffixes

   c) Nouns ending in a *vowel* + -*o* add -*s* to form the plural.

Singular	Plural
radio	radios
rodeo	rodeos
stereo	stereos
studio	studios
zoo	zoos

   d) Nouns ending in a *consonant* + -*o* follow no rule. These plural forms must be memorized as you consult your dictionary.

Singular	Plural
auto	autos
piano	pianos

   but

Singular	Plural
tomato	tomatoes
potato	potatoes
tornado	tornadoes

   e) Most nouns ending in -*f* or -*fe* form their plurals by changing the -*f* to -*v* and adding -*es*. If in doubt, use your dictionary.

Singular	Plural
knife	knives
wife	wives
leaf	leaves
calf	calves

   Note: These are exceptions.

hoof	hoofs or hooves
roof	roofs
belief	beliefs
the Toronto Maple Leafs	

f) Some nouns do not follow any of the above rules. These are irregular forms and they must be memorized.

Singular	Plural	Singular	Plural
man	men	sheep	sheep
woman	women	moose	moose
child	children	species	species
ox	oxen	foot	feet
deer	deer	tooth	teeth

g) Some nouns, often of Greek or Latin origin, retain their original plural form. These forms are irregular in English and must be memorized.

Singular	Plural	Singular	Plural
bas*is*	bas*es*	curricul*um*	curricul*a*
cris*is*	cris*es*	dat*um*	dat*a*
parenthes*is*	parenthes*es*	medi*um*	medi*a*
addend*um*	addend*a*	podi*um*	podi*a*
bacteri*um*	bacteri*a*	criteri*on*	criteri*a*

2. **Possessives**

Possessive nouns are discussed in connection with the use of the apostrophe. (See *Apostrophes, page 106*.)

Adjectives and Adverbs

The term *comparison* is used to refer to adjectives and adverbs that show degrees of intensity. The degrees are called *positive, comparative, and superlative*. Here is a chart that shows how the comparative and superlative forms of adjectives and adverbs are formed:

Comparison of Adjectives

Positive	Comparative	Superlative	Rule
warm	warmer	warmest	For most adjectives add *-er* for the comparative and add *-est* for the superlative. (See also *Spelling, page 84*.)
wet	wetter	wettest	
simple	simpler	simplest	
happy	happier	happiest	
kindly	kindlier	kindliest	
beautiful	more beautiful	most beautiful	For most adjectives of more than one syllable, use *more* to form the comparative, *most* to form the superlative.
gruesome	more gruesome	most gruesome	
difficult	more difficult	most difficult	
good	better	best	The comparative and superlative forms of some common adjectives are irregular. *These must be memorized.*
bad	worse	worst	
little	less	least	
much	more	most	
many	more	most	

Comparison of Adverbs

Positive	Comparative	Superlative	Rule
fast	faster	fastest	Add -*er* for the comparative and -*est* for the superlative to most adverbs not ending in -*ly*.
sweetly	more sweetly	most sweetly	Add *more* for the comparative and *most* for the superlative to most adverbs ending in -*ly*.
slowly	more slowly	most slowly	
greedily	more greedily	most greedily	
well	better	best	The comparative and superlative forms of some common adverbs are irregular. *These must be memorized*.
badly	worse	worst	
little	less	least	

Verbs Each verb has three principal parts. A common regular verb is *work*. Its principal parts are *work* (basic form), *worked* (past tense), and *worked* (past participle):

- I *work* hard.
- I *worked* hard yesterday.
- I have *worked* hard in the past year.

Notice how the past tense and the past participle are both formed by adding -*ed* to the basic form. All regular verbs follow this rule.

Many common verbs, however, are not regular. Their past tense and past participle forms cannot be made by simply adding -*ed* to the basic form. Here is a partial list of the principal parts of some common irregular verbs. Use your dictionary if you are unsure of a form. (See also *Using the Dictionary, page 82*.)

Basic form	Past tense	Past participle
arise	arose	arisen
begin	began	begun
blow	blew	blown
choose	chose	chosen
do	did	done
eat	ate	eaten
fly	flew	flown
give	gave	given
go	went	gone
hit	hit	hit
know	knew	known
lend	lent	lent
mistake	mistook	mistaken
pay	paid	paid
ring	rang	rung
see	saw	seen
shrink	shrank or shrunk	shrunk
string	strung	strung
think	thought	thought
throw	threw	thrown
write	wrote	written

As a general guideline:

- Memorize irregular forms as you learn them.
- Consult a dictionary whenever you are uncertain about form or usage.

Test yourself:
Which words in the following sentences are *not* in the correct form? What is the correct form?

1. Today, all children should learn to cook. In many familys, both husbands and wifes share in meal preparation. Gone are the days when men could get away with knowing how to make only a few dishs.

2. Too, people are using less freezed food. Basic ingredients like potatos and tomatos have found their way back into our diets.

3. Of course, foods that have already been prepared by manufacturers are often easyer to prepare, but they are not necessarily better than home-made foods. Mostly, they are selecting because they are sure to reach the table more soon than homemade foods.

4. When TV dinners first hit the market, they were sweeped off the supermarket shelves by eager buyers. But gradually, people found that these items were expensiver than the same meals made from scratch.

USAGE: COMMON WORD MIX-UPS

Many spelling and usage errors result from the confusion of pairs or groups of words that *look* alike or *sound* alike but are really quite different from one another in spelling and meaning. This chart shows some of the most common word mix-ups:

Words	Examples	Meanings
accept	The team *accepted* the trophy.	verb meaning "receive"
except	Everyone *except* Bill was at hockey practice.	preposition meaning "but"
advice	Do you want my *advice*?	noun meaning "suggestion"
advise	I *advise* you to stop smoking.	verb meaning "offer a suggestion"
affect	Nervousness *affected* my performance.	verb meaning "cause a change"
effect	Nervousness had a disastrous *effect* on my performance.	noun meaning "the result of a change"
choose	We always *choose* our own speech topics.	verb, present tense, meaning "select"
chose	Last semester, I *chose* to speak on the importance of energy conservation.	verb, past tense, meaning "selected"

coarse	The artist made a *coarse* preparatory sketch.	adjective meaning "rough, crude, not fine"
course	My brother is taking a *course* in philosophy at the university this term.	has several meanings but used only as a noun or a verb
desert	The frightened soldier *deserted* his companions in the *desert*.	verb meaning "abandon"; noun meaning "a dry region"
dessert	On my birthday, we had spice cake for *dessert*.	noun meaning "sweet food served after a meal"
hear	I always *hear* the bell.	verb meaning "perceive sound through the ear"
here	Set up your projector *here*.	adverb meaning "in this place"
its	A flower turns *its* blossom toward the sun.	possessive pronoun meaning "belonging to it"
it's	*It's* essential for the entire plant to have light.	contraction meaning "it is"
lead	These pipes are made of *lead*.	noun meaning "a kind of metal"
lead	*Lead* us to the auditorium.	verb, present tense, meaning "guide"
led	We *led* the visitors to the auditorium.	verb, past tense, meaning "guided"
loose	Set the animal *loose*.	adjective meaning "not fixed or fastened" (rhymes with *goose*)
lose	Do not *lose* your keys.	verb meaning "misplace"
of	This is a dictionary *of* literary terms.	functions only as a preposition
've	Rosalie wished she could*'ve* recopied her exam paper.	contraction of the verb *have*
our	How do you like *our* science display?	possessive adjective meaning "belonging to us"
are	*Are* you going to the concert?	form of the verb "be"
passed	As the parade *passed* by, the clowns *passed* out balloons to the children in the crowd.	verb meaning "went by" or "gave"

past	In the *past*, this highway was just a dirt road.	noun or adjective meaning "the time before the present"
	We drove *past* the school.	adverb meaning "beyond, farther than"
principal	Ms. Montclair is the *principal* of our school.	noun meaning "chief person", adjective meaning "chief"
principle	Scientific discovery is based on established *principles*.	noun meaning "a basic truth or belief"
quiet	Please be *quiet* in the library.	adjective, noun or verb meaning "not making sound"
quite	He has not *quite* finished.	adverb meaning "completely"
quit	Please *quit* shouting at me.	verb meaning "stop"
sole	I ordered *sole* for dinner because it was the *sole* item on the menu I recognized.	noun meaning "bottom part of a shoe" or "a flat ocean fish"; adjective meaning "single" or "only"
soul	Some people believe that the *soul* lives on after the body.	noun meaning "the part of a person distinct from the body" or simply "a person"
stationary	Heavy equipment is usually *stationary*.	adjective meaning "not moving"
stationery	I always get *stationery* from my grandmother for Christmas.	noun meaning "writing paper"
than	Mac is quicker with numbers *than* I am	conjunction or preposition showing comparison
then	I got out my biology book, but *then* I decided I'd rather watch television than study.	adverb meaning "at that time" or "next"
their	Mammals nurse *their* young.	possessive adjective meaning "belonging to them"
there	Put your hockey equipment over *there*.	adverb meaning "in that place"
they're	*They're* the first people in line.	contraction meaning "they are"
through	We drove *through* the Rockies on our vacation.	functions only as a preposition
threw	The catcher *threw* the ball to first.	verb, past tense, meaning "hurled" or "tossed"

to	I go *to* my piano lesson every Tuesday.	functions only as a preposition
too	I, *too*, ate *too* much pizza.	adverb meaning "also" and "more than enough"
two	Luigi can speak *two* languages fluently.	adjective or noun meaning "one more than one"
weather	Outdoor games are more enjoyable in fine *weather*.	noun meaning "condition of the atmosphere"
whether	She didn't know *whether* to laugh or to cry.	conjunction used to introduce a choice
were	The early settlers *were* immigrants from many countries.	past tense of "are", form of the verb "be"
where	*Where* did the settlers from France first make their homes?	adverb meaning "in what place"
which	*Which* province grows the most wheat?	functions only as a pronoun or adjective
witch	Without *witches*, some fairy tales would be dreary stories.	noun meaning "woman supposed to have magical powers"
who's	*Who's* playing the part of Hamlet?	contraction meaning "who is" or "who has"
whose	I know *whose* script this is.	possessive pronoun for "who" and "which"
your	*Your* cattle broke the fence.	possessive adjective meaning "belonging to you"
you're	*You're* going to have to pay for the repair of the fence.	contraction meaning "you are"

As a general guideline:

- Make sure each word you write expresses each word you think.
- Consult your dictionary frequently for spelling and usage.
- Refer to the above chart.

Test yourself:

Each of the following sentences contains at least one "word mix-up" error. Find the errors, then supply the correct words.

1. All accept a few of the world's zoos are more humane today then they were in passed years.

2. Specially trained people our available to advice zoo personnel, who's job it is too care for the animals.

3. In most facilities, its possible for the animals to run lose in quit large areas whenever they chose.

4. Of coarse, your likely two see the odd animal in a cage, but chances are its their for observation on the orders of a veterinarian.

WORD DIVISION (SYLLABICATION)

The best rule for word division, or syllabication, is to do it as rarely as possible in written work. If you *must* divide a word at the end of a line, here are some guidelines to follow.

1. **Between Syllables**

   Always divide between syllables and always place the hyphen at the end of the first line. Never begin a line with a hyphen.

   Avoid: A St. Thomas, Ontario, jewe
   -ller invented a painless way
   to pierce ears.

   Acceptable: The MP argued that environ-
   mental controls were the only
   answer to the problem.

2. **Short Words**

   Avoid dividing short words.

   Avoid: a- way
   heav- y
   brok- en
   sing- ing

   Acceptable: scien- tific
   philo- sophical
   docu- mentation
   inappro- priate

3. **Hyphenated Words**

   In hyphenated words, divide *only* at the hyphen.

   absent- minded
   good- natured
   soft- spoken
   twenty- seven

4. **Proper Nouns**

   Avoid dividing proper nouns.

   Avoid: Minis-try of Health
   Ali-son Gilbert

   Acceptable: University of British Columbia
   Margaret van Elsen

As a general guideline:

- Try not to divide words at all, but when you must, make sure both parts of the divided word are recognizable and pronounceable.

Test yourself:

Which of the following words would you divide at the end of a line? Why or why not? Where would you make the divisions?

1. easy-going
2. run
3. quantity
4. William
5. looking
6. sourdough

ABBREVIATION

Abbreviations should rarely be used in formal written assignments, especially where there may be confusion over their meaning.

Here are some common abbreviations that should be avoided in formal writing:

Avoid	Acceptable
etc.	and so on *or* and so forth
e.g.	for example
i.e.	that is
Xmas	Christmas
Sept. 14/53	14 September 1953
Fri., Sat.	Friday, Saturday
Eng., Hist.	English, History
The p. m. of Gr. Br. lives at 10 Downing St.	The prime minister of Great Britain lives at 10 Downing Street.

Here are the five kinds of abbreviations that *are* usually desirable in written work:

1. **Before Proper Names**

   Abbreviate titles *before* proper names. The most common abbreviations are

   > Mr., Mrs., Ms., Dr., Messrs., Mme., M.

2. **After Proper Names**

   Abbreviate titles and professional degrees *after* proper names. Some of the most common abbreviations are

   > Jr., Sr., B.A., M.D., Ph.D., D.D.S.

Do not use more than one abbreviation to convey the same meaning.

Avoid:	Dr. N. Osborne, M.D.
Acceptable:	Dr. N. Osborne
Acceptable:	N. Osborne, M.D.

3. **Agencies and Organizations**

Abbreviate names of government agencies and organizations when the abbreviations are more commonly used than the spelled-out names. Some examples are:

R.C.M.P.	NATO
Y.M.C.A.	UNICEF
U.N.	UNESCO

The trend is toward omitting the periods in such abbreviations, but consult the dictionary to be sure.

4. **"Saint"**

Abbreviate the word Saint when it is part of a place name.

St. John's, Newfoundland

St. Thomas, Ontario

but Saint John, New Brunswick

5. **Miscellaneous**

In certain kinds of papers and assignments, abbreviations of sums of money, times of the day, and units of measurement are accepted. As a rule of thumb, if there are a great many such references in the paper, abbreviations are probably best.

Money	$41.70
Time	9:30 a.m., 11:15 p.m.
	09:30, 23:15 (twenty-four-hour clock)

Measurement 16 km, 454 g, 6 mL

Note: Do not use periods after metric symbols, unless they come at the ends of sentences.

As a general guideline:

- Abbreviate titles used with proper names and commonly abbreviated names of organizations.

- Use other abbreviations only when that *type* of abbreviation appears several times in the paper and when the meaning of the abbreviation will be perfectly clear.

Test yourself:

If you were writing a formal paragraph or essay for an assignment, which abbreviations in the following sentences would you write differently? How would you write them?

1. On Sun. Dec. 7/41, the Japanese bombed Pearl Harbor.

2. U.S. Pres. Roosevelt immediately declared war on Japan.

3. Canada was already at war with the Germans, but the attack made Xmas even sadder that year.

4. From St. John to Vancouver, Canadians experienced hardships in WWII; rationing, the draft, bad news, etc. made life difficult.

NUMBERS AND METRIC UNITS

Numbers

In formal writing, numbers are generally spelled out unless a great many numbers are used in a single paper, such as a science paper. Here are three general rules for numbers:

1. **Numbers Below 101**

   Numbers below 101 are usually spelled out.
   Compound numbers between twenty-one and ninety-nine are hyphenated.

   > ninety-six kilometres
   >
   > sixteen players
   >
   > 135 cars

   Note: Round numbers over 101 are usually spelled out. For example, *two hundred* books, *a thousand* people.

2. **Numerals**

   Numerals may be used for dates, street numbers, room numbers, sums of money, telephone numbers, temperature readings, page numbers, numbered sections and chapters in books, statistics, and with *a.m.* and *p.m.* to indicate time.

   > 11 February 1940 *or* 11 02 40
   >
   > 6622 Elmwood Avenue
   >
   > 25°C (*not* 25 degrees Celsius)
   >
   > page 92, Chapter III

3. **Beginning a Sentence**

   When a number begins a sentence, it should be spelled out.

   > *Two hundred sixty-four* women and men sit in the House of Commons in Ottawa.

Metric Units

The following chart outlines the metric units in everyday use.

Quantity	Unit	Symbol
mass (weight)	gram (one-thousandth of kilogram) kilogram tonne (one thousand kilograms)	g kg t
volume and capacity	cubic centimetre cubic metre millilitre (one-thousandth of a litre) centilitre (one-hundredth of a litre) litre	cm^3 m^3 mL cL L

length	millimetre (one-thousandth of a metre)	mm
	centimetre (one-hundredth of a metre)	cm
	metre	m
	kilometre (one thousand metres)	km
area	hectare	ha
	square centimetre	cm^2
	square metre	m^2
speed	metres per second	m/s
	kilometres per hour	km/h
time	second	s
	minute	min
	hour	h
temperature	degree(s) Celsius	°C
pressure	pascal	Pa
	kilopascal (one thousand pascals)	kPa

Keep the following points in mind when you use metric measurement:

1. Avoid mixing numerals and the full names of metric symbols.

   Avoid: I bought *3 kilograms* of meat.

   Acceptable: I bought *3 kg* of meat.

   Acceptable: I bought *three kilograms* of meat.

2. Avoid using a period after a metric symbol (unless the symbol is at the end of a sentence).

   Avoid: There are over *11 000 000 ha.* of wheat in Canada.

   Acceptable: There are over *11 000 000* ha of wheat in Canada.

3. Use a hyphen between the numeral and the symbol when they are used as a modifier.

   Avoid: My car has a *300 cm^3* engine.

   Acceptable: My car has a *300-cm^3* engine.

4. Use decimals rather than fractions in metric units.

   Avoid: Joanne's height is $1^2/_3$ m.

As a general guideline:

- Numerals are most acceptable in math and science assignments and usually less appropriate in English, history, and social studies assignments.

- Use numerals only when a great many appear in your paper or when the spelled-out form appears long and awkward.

Test yourself:

Imagine that the sentences below have been taken from a social studies essay. Where numerals appear, decide whether or not they are in the best form. Change the form of the numerals whenever you think it will improve the quality of presentation for the essay.

1. The agricultural industry has changed dramatically over the past 50 years. By the year 1990, much of our produce may well be grown by methods unheard of as few as 10 years ago.

2. Some farmers report that they can produce one hundred forty-five bushels of corn on exactly the same land that brought their fathers only forty five bushels 35 years ago.

3. However, this trend toward ever greater yields is levelling off. These same farmers report zero increase in yield over the past 5 years.

CAPITAL LETTERS

1. In General

Capitalize the first word of a sentence, the pronoun *I*, and proper nouns.

Example	Category
My father says I ought to improve my penmanship.	first word in sentence and pronoun I
Alice Munro, Jane Browne, Rover, Rin Tin Tin	names of people and animals
Vancouver, Hudson Bay	geographical locations
Tuesday, June, New Year's Day	days, months, and holidays
Social Studies 20	specific school courses
Canada Packers, Inc., Red Cross	names of companies and organizations
Irish, Caucasian, Yiddish	nationalities, races, and languages
Buddhism, Christianity	religions
CN Tower	buildings
10532 - 92 Avenue	parts of addresses

2. Direct Quotation

Capitalize the first word in a direct quotation.

"Tomorrow morning," announced Ms. Williams, "*we'll* have a short test on long division."

Note: The word *we'll* is not capitalized because it does not begin a sentence.

3. Historical

Capitalize the names of historical events and documents.

World War II, the British North America Act

4. Titles

Capitalize the first word and all important words in the titles of books, movies, plays, songs, articles, poems, and short stories.

The Call of the Wild, "An Ounce of Cure", *Star Wars*

5. **Letters**

Capitalize the first word in the salutation and closing of a letter.

Dear Abby, Dear Mr. Glen, Yours truly, Sincerely

6. **Titles Before Names**

Capitalize titles before the names of individuals.

Rabbi Morris, Ambassador Rodriguez, Mrs. Mathews

Give the prescription to Doctor Jones.

Note: Titles that are used alone are not capitalized.

The doctor gave me a prescription.

When in doubt, check your dictionary.

7. **Other**

Capitalize words like *father, mother,* and *uncle* when they are part of a person's name or when they are used in place of a person's name.

"Why don't you ask Mum?"

I enjoy hunting with Uncle Walter.

but

My father and uncle play on the same hockey team.

Note: Do not capitalize *north, south, east, west,* or any combination of these unless they are part of a proper name, such as *North York* or *South Dakota.* Do not capitalize the seasons: *spring, summer, fall, autumn, winter.*

As a general guideline:

- Do not use capital letters casually or for effect.
- Remember that they are most often used for names of *specific* people, things, and events, and at the beginning of a sentence.

Test yourself:

There are a number of capitalization errors in the following sentences. Revise the sentences.

1. Surely my Uncle didn't intend to fight the battle of the plains of abraham again!
2. "we're going to meet general Montcalm and his forces," said uncle françois, "And this time we'll win the battle."
3. The seven years' war would never have ended as it did if my crazy uncle had been fighting.
4. as he often says, Someone could then have written a book called the five days' war.

PUNCTUATION

Period The primary use of the period is to end statements or commands.

> "Googol" is the mathematical term for the number one followed by one hundred zeros.
>
> Memorize the symbols on the periodic table of the elements.

Periods are also frequently used in abbreviations. (See also *Abbreviation, page 97*.)

Note: Do not use periods after metric symbols; for example, 10 mL, 31 m, 25 L. If a metric symbol is at the end of a sentence, there will be a period to close the sentence.

> He ran 1500 m.

Comma Whenever you are unsure about comma usage, first check the rules in this section; however, "When in doubt, leave it out."

1. **Lists**

   Use a comma to separate the items in a series or list.

   > In Greek mythology, Zeus, Hera, Ares, Pallas Athena, and Apollo made their home on Mount Olympus.
   >
   > The salami rolled out of the yard, between two parked cars, and onto the road.

   Note: The comma before the conjunction, as in ". . . Pallas Athena, and Apollo . . ." is optional. But whichever method you choose, be consistent throughout a piece of writing.

2. **Introductory Words or Groups of Words**

   a) Use a comma after introductory words such as "No", "Well", "However", and so on.

   > Well, what did you discover?
   >
   > Nevertheless, we had a great time at the party.

   b) A phrase at the beginning of a sentence should be followed by a comma if it is long or if its meaning may be misunderstood.

   > Because the organizers feared a rainstorm, the game was postponed for a week.
   >
   > Speeding up, the car swung out to pass the truck.

3. **Words of Address**

   Words of address should be set off by commas.

   > George, did you understand that part about multiplying exponents?
   >
   > I didn't understand it at all, Mr. Green.
   >
   > Dear Joan,

4. **Additional Information**

A comma should be used to mark off additional, but not essential, information about a noun that comes before the information.

> My sister, who has red hair, is wearing a brown dress.

5. **Interruption of Thought**

Use a comma to mark the interruption of a thought.

> The teacher, needless to say, did not overlook Jill's failure to follow directions.

6. **Conjunctions**

Use a comma before a conjunction (such as *and, but,* or *or*) that joins two parts of a compound sentence.

> John is a very good student, and he is also an excellent athlete.

Question Mark

The question mark is used to end sentences that ask a question.

> Will we have to include footnotes?
>
> How long does the speech have to be?

Exclamation Mark

The exclamation mark is used after sentences showing surprise or strong feeling. Use this punctuation sparingly or it will lose its meaning.

> Henry Ford didn't invent the automobile!
>
> I certainly would not call that man a liberal!

Colon

The colon is not needed very often. Chiefly, it is used to introduce items or ideas.

1. **Lists**

Use a colon to begin a list of items.

> Bring these items: a pen, lined paper, a protractor, and your textbook.

Do not use colons after verbs and prepositions.

> **Avoid:** Bring: a pen, lined paper, a protractor, and your textbook.
>
> The neighbour accused the dog of: barking after midnight, chasing his cat, and burying bones in his yard.

2. **Quotations**

Use a colon to separate introductory words from a formal quotation that is a complete sentence.

> Stephen Leacock's most famous line is often quoted: "Lord Ronald said nothing; he flung himself from the room, flung himself upon his horse and rode madly off in all directions."

3. **Business Letters**

Use a colon after the greeting of a business letter.

> Dear Mrs. McDonnell:
>
> Dear Messrs. Adamson and Ohira:
> (See also *Business Letters, page 123*.)

4. **Time**

When numerals are used to express time, use a colon to separate the hours and minutes.

> The bus leaves at 3:10 p.m.
>
> The bus leaves at 15:10.

5. **Plays**

Use a colon between act and scene numbers of a play.

> Shakespeare's *Hamlet*, III:ii

6. **The Bible**

Use a colon between chapter and verse numbers of the Bible.

> Genesis 2:17

7. **References**

Use a colon between volume and page numbers of a reference that is cited.

> *Literary History of Canada*, II:179

8. **Subtitles**

Use a colon to introduce a subtitle of a book or article, or to introduce a section in one of these.

> "Changing Aberdeen: The North Sea Oil Boom" (article)

Semicolon

A semicolon is a tricky piece of punctuation. It is often described as both a strong comma and a weak period because it is used to join and separate parts of a sentence. Since the usage of the semicolon cannot be clearly defined, it is used sparingly and usually only in formal writing.

1. A semicolon is used to connect two complete thoughts if no joining word (such as *and* or *but*) is used. The two thoughts should be closely related to each other. The second thought does not begin with a capital letter.

> The results of the experiment were disappointing; our attempt to turn ginger ale into oil had failed completely.

2. A semicolon can be used before joining words such as *however, consequently, therefore*, and *nevertheless*.

> Mr. Scrooge is certainly a fictional character; nevertheless, in the minds of many, he has become as real as any historical figure one might care to name.

Dash   The dash may sometimes be used in informal writing and in dialogue, but rarely in formal writing. It should always be used sparingly. Use a dash *only* to mark a sudden change in sentence structure or a break in thought.

> The NHL uses about 15 000 pucks a year — enough to form a stack 440 m high.

Note: In typing, a dash is often shown as two hyphens so that it will not be mistaken for a hyphen. In writing, it should be slightly longer than a hyphen.

Hyphen   The hyphen is used to divide a word at the end of a line and to spell certain words correctly. (See *Hyphenated Words, page 87* and *Word Division, page 96*.)

Apostrophe   The apostrophe shows possession and replaces missing letters in contractions.

1. **Possession**

   a) To show possession of singular nouns, add *-'s*.

   > the school's book, Mark's speech

   b) To show possession of plural nouns *not* ending in *-s*, add *-'s*.

   > the men's department, the mice's tails

   c) To show possession of plural nouns ending in *-s*, add only an apostrophe.

   > the boys' books (more than one book belonging to more than one boy)
   >
   > the teachers' lounge (one lounge belonging to more than one teacher)

   d) *Do not* use an apostrophe or an *-'s* to show possession for the pronoun *who* or for personal pronouns. Here is a list of these pronouns with their correct possessive forms:

Pronouns	Possessive
I	mine
you	yours
he, she, it	his, hers, its
we	ours
you	yours
they	theirs
who	whose
but	
one	one's
everybody	everybody's

2. **Contractions**

   An apostrophe is inserted in a contraction to mark where one or more letters have been removed. Avoid contractions in formal writing. However, contractions may be used in certain assignments where it is appropriate to write in an informal or conversational style. They may also be used when writing dialogue.

Here are some common contractions. The apostrophe is used to mark the omission of the underlined letters.

do not	don't
cannot	can't
should have	should've
it is	it's
who is	who's

Quotation Marks

Quotation marks are usually used to separate someone's exact speech from the body of the work. In certain situations they are used to emphasize words and phrases that are not speech. The following show the most common uses.

1. **Direct Speech**

   Quotation marks are used to enclose a speaker's exact words. Use them only in writing direct speech, not in writing indirect speech.

   Direct Speech: The old gentleman said, "I think Sir John A. Macdonald was a great Canadian."

   Indirect Speech: The old gentleman said he thought Sir John A. Macdonald was a great Canadian.

   a) If the direct speech asks a question, the question mark is placed inside the quotation marks.

      The old gentleman said, "Do you think Sir John A. Macdonald was a great Canadian?"

   b) If the entire sentence asks a question, the question mark is placed *outside* the quotation marks.

      Did the old gentleman say, "I think Sir John A. Macdonald was a great Canadian"?

      Note: No period is shown after the direct speech.

2. **Dialogue**

   Quotation marks are used to mark the exact words of different speakers in a conversation. The following passage illustrates most of the rules for punctuating dialogue.

Indent each new paragraph.

Whole sentence is a question. Question mark goes inside quotation mark.

Each sentence of speech must begin and end with quotation marks.

New paragraph for each new speaker.

Use a comma, not a period.

New sentence follows. Use a period.

"I don't believe it," said Josie flatly. "I don't believe anybody could walk a ridgepole. *You* couldn't, anyhow."

"Couldn't I?" cried Anne rashly.

"Then I dare you to do it," said Jose defiantly. "I dare you to climb up there and walk the ridgepole of Mr. Barry's kitchen roof."

Anne turned pale, but there was clearly only one thing to be done. She walked toward the house, where a ladder was leaning against the kitchen roof. All the girls said "Oh!", partly in excitement, partly in dismay.

"Don't you do it, Anne," entreated Diana. "You'll fall off and be killed. Never mind Josie Pye. It isn't fair to dare anybody to do anything so dangerous."

"I must do it. My honour is at stake," said Anne solemnly. "I shall walk on that ridgepole, Diana, or perish in the attempt. If I am killed you are to have my pearl bead ring."

(From *Anne of Green Gables* by L. M. Montgomery)

Note: If a speaker's comment is longer than one paragraph, begin each paragraph with a quotation mark. Place a quotation mark only at the end of the *last* paragraph of the entire quotation.

For a quotation within a quotation, use single quotation marks.

Joe exclaimed, "Didn't you hear her? She said, 'Study the last chapter for a quiz tomorrow.' "

3. **Quotations in an Essay**

Quotation marks are used to enclose material that is a direct duplication of another writer's words. You will probably have occasion to use them in this way in research papers. You may also want to quote several authors in an essay.

Dance has increasingly become a topic of popular interest. Twenty years ago, "most people could not name a noted contemporary dancer." [1] Today, most Canadians know that Karen Kain is an international ballet star, although most acclaimed dancers are still not household names. Of particular significance is the diversity of interest: "Ballet, modern dance, and ballroom dancing are just some of the dance-styles that are in the public eye." [2] Whether it is part of an exercise program or an evening's entertainment, dance is becoming an important part of Canadian life.

Note: The number after each quotation refers to a footnote. (See also *Footnotes, page 54.*)

4. **Long Quotations**

Quotations of more than four lines are considered to be *long quotations*. Quotation marks are *not* used to mark long quotations. Instead, the entire quotation is indented twice the normal paragraph indent on both sides and single-spaced.

> For centuries, people have been fascinated by the phrase "the secret of life". In 1953, two men discovered that secret.
>
> > How the message of inheritance is passed from one generation to the next was discovered in 1953, and it is the adventure story of science in the twentieth century. I suppose the moment of drama is the autumn of 1951, when a young man in his twenties, James Watson, arrives in Cambridge and teams up with a man of thirty-five, Francis Crick, to decipher the structure of deoxyribonucleic acid, DNA for short.[1]
>
> So dramatic was the impact of Watson and Crick's discovery that genetics is today one of the most exciting and controversial branches of science.
>
> _____
> [1] J. Bronowski, *The Ascent of Man* (London: British Broadcasting Corporation, 1973), p. 390.

5. **Quotation Within a Quotation**

If the original writer whom you are quoting has *already* included quoted material in his or her sentence, change the original quotation marks to single quotation marks and use regular quotation marks to enclose the passage as a whole.

> The Shakespearian critic James Smith suggests that "Hamlet's 'To be or not to be' speech is the key to the character's philosophy."

6. **Titles**

Quotation marks are used to enclose the titles of magazine and newspaper articles, book chapters, poems, songs, short stories, and essays.

"Inside the Saudi Royal Family"	(magazine article)
"Practical Applications of Geometry"	(book chapter)
"The Vagabonds"	(poem title)
"O Canada"	(song title)

7. **For Emphasis**

Quotation marks are used to draw attention to specific words that they enclose. Often, this use is made prior to a definition or an explanation of the quoted word by the writer.

> Don't use the word "and" so frequently.
>
> When I ask for the "etymology" of a given word, I want a listing of the forms from which the word is derived.

Note: Sometimes underlining or italics are used in place of quotation marks in situations like the ones illustrated above. Be consistent. Choose one of the methods and use it throughout a piece of writing.

Parentheses   Parentheses are used to enclose supplementary explanations and comments so that they do not become confused with the overall flow of thought. Parentheses should be used *very* sparingly in school assignments.

1. **For Part of a Sentence**

   If the parentheses appear within a sentence, do *not* begin the material inside the parentheses with a capital letter.

   > The summer concert will be held in the auditorium on June 20 (the last day of school).

   Note: The period in the above sentence is *outside* the last parenthesis. That is because the period ends the whole sentence, not just the material within the parentheses.

2. **For an Entire Sentence**

   If parentheses are used to enclose an entire sentence, place the period *inside* the final parenthesis.

   > Bill frowned when we asked him to referee the game (He always frowns when we ask for his help.) but he did it anyway.

   Note: Square brackets are used to insert editorial comments in quotations. Editorial comment may involve changing a word or two in the quotation so it will read properly or adding supplementary information such as names and dates.

   > "Eaton's used to turn a big part of their store into a toyland at Christmas time and that year, the Shirley Temple year, they had these dolls [of the young Hollywood star] along one end of the toyland."
   >
   > (From *Ten Lost Years* by Barry Broadfoot)

Ellipsis Marks   Ellipsis marks are used to show that something has been left out of a quotation. The part omitted may be as short as a single word or as long as several sentences. Ellipsis marks are three spaced periods that take the place of the omitted material. Do not use ellipsis marks to alter the meaning of a quotation.

Full Quotation: The actor said, "Playing the title role in *Hamlet*, despite the acclaim of the audience, is very tiring for me."

Quotation using Ellipsis Marks: The actor said, "Playing the title role in *Hamlet* . . . is very tiring for me."

Note: If the ellipsis is used at the end of a sentence, include the period that would normally come at the end of the sentence. Thus instead of three ellipsis marks, there would be four.

Underlining and Italics Underlining is used in longhand or typewritten assignments, wherever italic type would be used in printed material.

1. **Titles**
   Underline the titles of books, magazines, newspapers, plays, and movies, as well as the names of specific ships or planes.

A Bird in the House	(book by Margaret Laurence)
Maclean's	(magazine)
The Vancouver Sun	(newspaper)
Cyclone Jack	(play by Carol Bolt)
Citizen Kane	(movie)
Titanic	(ship)

2. **Emphasis**
   a) Underlining may be used very sparingly instead of an exclamation mark to emphasize a specific word in a sentence.

      That is definitely not the best way to handle the problem.

   b) Underlining is used for foreign words or phrases. If in doubt, consult your dictionary.

      beaux-arts
      deus ex machina

As a general guideline:

- Most punctuation marks are used to separate or end thoughts for the reader.

- Every punctuation mark should make writing easier, not harder, to understand.

Test yourself:

1. There are many punctuation errors in the following paragraph. Change whatever punctuation marks you think are incorrect and add any that you think are missing.

   What would you say is the twentieth centurys greatest contribution to literature. If youre like most people after a moment's thought youll probably say science fiction." Surprisingly this common answer is not precisely correct it's only half right. The reason why this answer is only half right is simple Two of the greatest science fiction writer's of all time did most of their's best writing before the year 1900. They are: Jules Verne and H. G. Wells. Verne's famous Twenty Thousand Leagues Under the Sea was published in 1870, Wells classic The Time Machine first appeared in 1895 and his terrifying The War of the Worlds came out in 1898.

2. Just for fun, here are grammar and style tips that somehow went wrong. Can you correct them? Can you add others?*

Verbs has to agree with their subjects.

Don't never use double negatives.

Avoid, commas, that are unnecessary.

Don't use run-on sentences they are hard to read.

Use all adverbs correct.

Everyone should be careful to use a singular pronoun with singular nouns in their writing.

Writing carefully, dangling modifiers must be avoided.

Check carefully to if you left any words out.

Spel correctly.

About sentence fragments.

Repeating and repeating a word over and over is not usually effective.

Take the bull by the horns to avoid those mixed metaphors that will slip through if you're not careful.

Last but not least, avoid clichés like the plague.

* based on material found in William Safire's *On Language*, Avon Books.

HANDWRITING

Handwriting that is difficult to read is annoying to the reader. If letters are carelessly formed, for example if *d* looks like *cl*, or *ci* looks like *a*, some words may be misunderstood.

1. Most handwriting problems can be avoided by paying attention to the following points:

   - Always close the tops of *a*, *d*, *g*, and *q*.
   - Make upper loops in *b*, *e*, *h*, *k*, and *l*.
   - *Do not* make upper loops in *i*, *d*, *j*, and *t*.
   - Keep the downstrokes straight in *h*, and *n*.
   - "Tie back" the second downstroke in *k*, *p*, and *s*.
   - Bring the downstrokes right to the base line in *a*, *d*, *h*, *k*, *m*, *n*, *v*, *u*, and *s*.
   - Remember to make a small point at the top of *v*, *w*, *n*, and *s*.

2. It is important to observe the following points, to give a pleasing appearance to your handwritten pages:

   - Maintain an even base line.
   - Make a clear distinction between short and tall letters.
   - Strive for uniformity in slant, height, size, and spacing.
   - Avoid extremes — writing that is very large or very small, or that slants far to the left or right.

- Do not crowd your writing. Strive for even spacing between letters and words.

- If you must make a correction on a page that cannot be rewritten, such as an exam paper, neatly cross out the incorrect word and write the correct word beside it or above it. Do not try to write over the mistake.

Here is a handwriting chart showing generally accepted ways of forming letters.

Aa	Bb	Cc	Dd
Ee	Ff	Gg	Hh
Ii	Jj	Kk	Ll
Mm	Nn	Oo	Pp
Qq	Rr	Ss	Tt
Uu	Vv	Ww	Xx
Yy	Zz	1234567890	
th	sh	ch	ck
ea	ae	ie	ei
wh	qu	bl	st
or	er	ir	ur
gh	ph	sp	fl
oo	str	spr	tt
rt	ft	sn	sm

CORRECTION MARKS

The symbols and abbreviations listed on the left side of this page are often used in marking student papers and may appear on your corrected papers. If you are not sure of the error you have made, locate the symbol and its meaning below and consult the appropriate section of this book for an explanation of your error and suggestions for avoiding it in the future. Also, use the *Index* in this book to look up specific items that may be noted on your corrected paper.

Symbol	Meaning	Page
para	new paragraph needed	52
no para	no paragraph needed	52
∧	word or phrase missing	112
p	punctuation error	103
apos	apostrophe error	106
CAP	capitalization error	101
quo	use of quotation marks	107
D	diction (imprecise, meaning unclear)	31
awk	awkward word order	69
usage	word usage error	92
sl	slang	36
inf	informal language	29
red	redundant	78
rep	repetitious	78
frag	not a sentence (fragment)	66
run-on	run-on sentence	66
sp	spelling error	84
vt	verb tense error	72
abb	abbreviate	97
agr	subject-verb agreement	70
d	word division error	96
mis	modifier mistake	67
pron	pronoun usage or agreement	74

CHAPTER 6
Letters

LETTERS

A letter can often be the best way of handling
certain situations. It may be to make a complaint,
to thank someone, or to get a job. While a letter
may be a good idea, if it is not well done it may
do more harm than good. This Chapter will help
you write the most effective letter for the occasion.

CONTENTS

APPLYING THE WRITING PROCESS

There are three basic kinds of letters:

- friendly letters
- business letters
- letters written to seek employment

This chapter provides guidelines and models for each type.

To write the best letter that you can, always follow the eight steps of the writing process. (See also *The Writing Process, page 16*.)

When writing a friendly letter, you may be able to take some of these points fairly casually or eliminate them altogether. For business letters and letters written to seek employment, follow each step just as you would for a school assignment. For all letters, pay special attention to Step 2, the three important aspects of good writing. Each letter you write will have a distinctive purpose and a distinctive audience. Use these points as a guide.

FRIENDLY LETTERS

Friendly letters are written to people you know more or less well. They can be "newsy" letters to relatives or close friends, or they can be short, slightly more formal notes to express thanks, sympathy, congratulations, or invitations. All friendly letters have two common features:

(a) They are informal, warm, and relaxed in tone.

(b) They are presented more or less in the format illustrated in the examples in this section. Friendly letters may be either typed or handwritten. Both types are shown here.

On the following pages are samples of friendly letters written for different occasions. Each letter is preceded by Step 2 of the writing process as a guide for that letter.

Sharing Information

This is an example of a friendly letter between people sharing the same interests and "language".

Purpose: to tell a friend some exciting news

Audience: a very close friend of my own age

Statement   I am writing an informal letter to a very close friend
of Purpose: to relate some exciting news.

- Slang and contractions are appropriate in this situation.
- Show interest in the person to whom you are writing.
- Other closings in a letter of this kind could be

    Your friend,
    Your loving friend,
    Your old pal,
    Yours ever,
    or anything you wish!

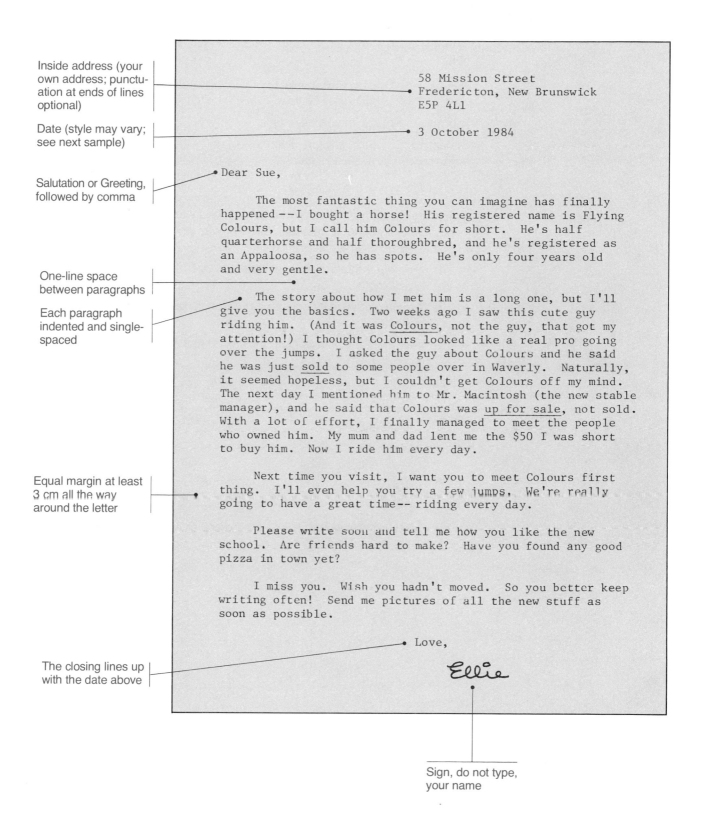

Inside address (your own address; punctuation at ends of lines optional)

Date (style may vary; see next sample)

Salutation or Greeting, followed by comma

One-line space between paragraphs

Each paragraph indented and single-spaced

Equal margin at least 3 cm all the way around the letter

The closing lines up with the date above

Sign, do not type, your name

58 Mission Street
Fredericton, New Brunswick
E5P 4L1

3 October 1984

Dear Sue,

The most fantastic thing you can imagine has finally happened --I bought a horse! His registered name is Flying Colours, but I call him Colours for short. He's half quarterhorse and half thoroughbred, and he's registered as an Appaloosa, so he has spots. He's only four years old and very gentle.

The story about how I met him is a long one, but I'll give you the basics. Two weeks ago I saw this cute guy riding him. (And it was Colours, not the guy, that got my attention!) I thought Colours looked like a real pro going over the jumps. I asked the guy about Colours and he said he was just sold to some people over in Waverly. Naturally, it seemed hopeless, but I couldn't get Colours off my mind. The next day I mentioned him to Mr. Macintosh (the new stable manager), and he said that Colours was up for sale, not sold. With a lot of effort, I finally managed to meet the people who owned him. My mum and dad lent me the $50 I was short to buy him. Now I ride him every day.

Next time you visit, I want you to meet Colours first thing. I'll even help you try a few jumps. We're really going to have a great time-- riding every day.

Please write soon and tell me how you like the new school. Are friends hard to make? Have you found any good pizza in town yet?

I miss you. Wish you hadn't moved. So you better keep writing often! Send me pictures of all the new stuff as soon as possible.

Love,

Ellie

Thank-You

This letter is completely different in purpose and audience from the preceding one. The tone is slightly more formal, yet it is still warm and relaxed. The format is identical to the one used above. Slang should not be used in letters of this type.

Purpose: to express thanks for a special weekend at my friend's parents' cottage

Audience: my friend's parents

Statement of Purpose: I am writing an informal but polite thank-you letter to my friend's parents.

Each paragraph in this thank-you note has a specific purpose:

- The first paragraph begins with a general and warm thank-you. The phrase "last weekend" tells that the letter was written promptly, as all thank-you notes and letters should be.

- The second paragraph names at least one specific reason why the thank-you is meaningfully given.

- The third paragraph is a concluding paragraph, underlining the sentiment of the letter.

- The fourth paragraph shows special interest in the people to whom the letter is written.

- Other closings for this type of letter could be

> Your friend,
> Sincerely,
> Yours respectfully,
> Yours affectionately,
> Best wishes,
> Regards,

depending on how well you know the person to whom you are writing.

35 Maya Road
Haltersville, Ontario
M7P 8N6.

January 20, 1985

Dear Mr. and Mrs. Schon,

Thank you very much for having me as a guest at your cottage last weekend. I had a wonderful time because all the things you and Rob planned were really special.

Most exciting was the snowshoeing, which I would never have a chance to do here in town. And, as I'm sure you noticed, pumpkin pie is my favourite!

It was a weekend I will long remember, and I thank you all for making me feel like a part of your family.

I hope you get your wish and are able to enjoy skiing right through until March.

Yours sincerely,

Mario

Sympathy

Purpose: to express sympathy for the death of my friend's father

Audience: a friend from school

Statement of Purpose: I am writing an informal but polite letter of sympathy to a friend from school.

- A letter of sympathy is difficult to write, but there is probably no time when an expression of concern is more appreciated.
- Write such a letter *promptly*.
- Be brief and sincere, but also be tactful in what you say. Avoid too much sentiment.
- Another type of closing in a letter of this kind could be

  Affectionately,

depending on how well you know the person to whom you are writing.

9106 - 82 Avenue
Charlottetown,
Prince Edward Island
C1T 5L1
March 22, 1999

Dear Bob,

I was very sorry to hear that your dad passed away the day before yesterday. He was a wonderful man and I will always remember what an inspiration he was for our team the summer we won the championship. I know I will miss him. My thoughts and prayers are with you and your family.

Yours sincerely,
Jim

Invitation

Purpose: to extend an invitation for a visit during spring break

Audience: a cousin who lives in Pictou

Statement of Purpose: I am writing an informal letter to invite my cousin to visit me during spring break.

- A letter of invitation asks the reader to visit a particular place or to engage in a particular activity at a specific time and place.
- Tell the reader immediately what the purpose of the invitation is. Do not forget to include any necessary details, such as date, place, length of invitation, and, if applicable, what to wear and what to bring.
- Indicate whether a reply is expected of the reader.

59 McDonald Drive
Truro, Nova Scotia
B2N 1L2
March 5, 1999

Dear Helena,
How would you like to come to my house during the spring break? Could you arrive on Friday afternoon March 24? You are welcome to stay the full ten days if you wish. Don't forget your riding clothes, swimsuit, and those records you received for your birthday.
Please let me know if you are able to come.
Your friend,
Laura

Acceptance

Purpose:	to accept an invitation for a visit during spring break
Audience:	a cousin who lives in Truro
Statement of Purpose:	I am writing an informal letter to my cousin to accept an invitation to visit her during spring break.

- A statement of acceptance shows appreciation for the invitation that has been extended.

- Avoid confusion by stating the date, time, and place of the event.

- Reply as quickly as possible to any invitation.

86 Deerfoot Trail
Picton, Nova Scotia
B3M 1J3
March 11, 1999

Dear Laura,
Your invitation to spend the spring break at your house couldn't have come at a better time. Since Dad can't get off work we were unable to make vacation plans of our own. I'm sure we'll have a great time riding horses and doing other things.
I'll be travelling on the Greyhound bus which leaves here at noon on Friday. I'm depending on your Dad to pick me up at the depot at two o'clock.
I'm so excited about it all!
All the best,
Helena

Decline   Purpose: to decline an invitation for a visit during spring break

Audience: a cousin who lives in Truro

Statement   I am writing an informal letter to my cousin to
of Purpose: decline an invitation to visit her during spring break.

- A letter declining an invitation shows appreciation for the invitation.
- Give the reason for not accepting the invitation.
- Express your best wishes to the person who has made the invitation.
- Reply as quickly as possible to any invitation.

> 86 Deerfoot Trail
> Picton, Nova Scotia
> B3M 1J3
>
> March 11, 1999
>
> Dear Laura,
>
>   I am very sorry that I cannot accept your invitation to spend the spring break with you. My family has already planned a trip to Disney World, and we will be gone for the full ten days.
>
>   I certainly appreciate the invitation and would be glad to visit you at another time. However, I hope you enjoy your holiday.
>
> Your friend,
> Helena

BUSINESS LETTERS

Business letters can be used to seek information, make requests, place orders for goods, check on orders already placed, make claims for damages, express political views, or express thanks (for example, to a guest speaker or an interview subject).

- All good business letters are formal, clear, concise, and complete in their presentation of the matter at hand.

- Every business letter should be on standard-sized 21.5 cm × 28.0 cm (8½″ × 11″) white paper and either written in ink or typed. (Both types are shown here.) Be very careful about grammar, spelling, and punctuation. (See also *Forms of Address, page 128*.)

- Suggested formats for business letters are illustrated in the following examples. The first example follows the format for typewritten business letters, while the second follows the format for handwritten business letters. There are other acceptable forms, but these are in common use today.

Seeking Information

Purpose:	to seek information on airport security as handled by the R.C.M.P. at the Montreal International Airport
Audience:	an official of the R.C.M.P.
Statement of Purpose:	I am writing a formal business letter seeking information on a specific topic from an official of the R.C.M.P.

The sample letter on the following page illustrates the pattern to follow in all your business letters:

- It is addressed to a specific person. Whenever possible, try to obtain a name before writing to a large organization.

- The first paragraph comes immediately to the point, stating exactly why the writer is writing.

- The tone of the letter is formal and polite, but neither flattering nor apologetic.

- The second-to-last paragraph defines the specific purpose of the letter so there can be no confusion as to how the recipient should reply.

- The last paragraph contains a sentence of "thanks in advance" and notes that a self-addressed, stamped envelope is enclosed. This step increases the chances of receiving a prompt answer.

- Some other acceptable closings for business letters:

    Yours very truly,
    Yours sincerely,
    Yours faithfully,
    Yours respectfully,

Writer's address and date

14 Garden Place
Cornwall, Ont. K6T 5B6

1985-04-30

Name and address of recipient at left margin

Staff Sergeant Alec Smedley
OC Airport Security
Montreal International Airport
Montreal, P.Q. G4N 2K4

Salutation followed by colon

Dear Staff Sergeant Smedley:

Each paragraph begins at left margin with no indent

Our Contemporary Studies class at Broadview High School
is presently studying the professional activities of the
R.C.M.P. in Canada. My particular area of research is
airport security as it applies to Montreal International
Airport.

Single-spaced except between paragraphs; one-line space between paragraphs

Inspector P. Garneau of C Division Headquarters in Montreal
indicated that you, as head of Airport Security, would be
the person most qualified to assist with my inquiries.

I would appreciate it very much if you would send me
information on airport security at your earliest
convenience or grant me an interview at a time convenient
to you.

Thank you for considering this request. I have enclosed
a self-addressed, stamped envelope for your reply.

Closing followed by a comma

Yours truly,

Space for signature

Lee Kaufman

Full name typed or printed; you may include Mr., Mrs., Miss, or Ms. in parentheses

(Mr.) Lee Kaufman

Request

Purpose: to obtain permission on behalf of my drama club to put on the play, *Leaving Home* by David French

Audience: Sage Productions, the formal representative of David French for this play, as noted in the front of the script (no specific name given)

Statement of Purpose: I am writing a formal business letter to Sage Productions to obtain permission to stage the play, *Leaving Home* by David French.

Writer's address and date at right margin

70 Jumping Pond Drive
Saskatoon, Saskatchewan
S7M 3P2

1986-11-29

Name and address of recipient at left margin

Sage Productions
30 Bridgman Avenue
Toronto, Ontario
M2R 3P6

Salutation followed by colon

Dear Sir or Madam:

Each paragraph begins at left margin with indent

Single-spaced

I am writing on behalf of the Drama Club at Laurier High School, for your permission to stage the play *Leaving Home* by David French.

We would like to hold seven performances, one each evening from Friday, March 11 through, Friday, March 18, excluding Sunday. The admission fee will be $2.00.

Would you please tell me the requirements for permission to stage this play and, let me know if you need any further information. If there is a charge for performing rights, please advise me as to your fee.

Enclosed is a self-addressed, stamped envelope for your reply. Thank you in advance for your attention to this matter. I look forward to hearing from you.

Closing followed by comma at right margin

Signature at right margin

Yours Sincerely,
Ivan S. Brodowski
Ivan S. Brodowski

Full name typed or printed; you may include Mr., Mrs., Miss, or Ms. in parentheses

Secretary,
Laurier High School Drama Club

Complaint

Purpose: to complain about the functioning of my 2B4B house-cleaning robot

Audience: sales manager of Never-Fail Robotics

Statement of Purpose: I am writing a formal letter of complaint to the sales manager of Never-Fail Robotics about the problems with my 2B4B housecleaning robot.

Almost everyone has occasion at one time or another to write a letter of complaint. Here are some points to remember:

- Address the letter to a specific department and individual (including his or her name, if you know it).
- Supply all the information you can about the item you are writing about — date of purchase, where purchased, model, serial number, and so on.
- State clearly the reason for your complaint.
- Keep the tone of the letter formal but polite.
- Make a copy of the letter and keep it for reference.

```
25 Spaceship Lane
New Terra, Andromeda
45BXFT679B-1

2056-08-30

Mr. James Brown, Sales Manager
Never-Fail Robotics
18 Galactica Avenue
New Canada, Earth
67HEFY595C-3

Dear Mr. Brown:

     On 2055-06-01, I purchased from your local outlet on
New Terra a model 2B4B housecleaning robot.  This robot has
never worked properly since I bought it.  Although I program
it to take out the garbage, it constantly spreads the garbage
over the basement floor.  When I program it to prepare dinner
for two, three, or four, it always multiplies that amount by
ten.  Do you know how disturbing it is to arrive home with
three guests from an exhausting day at the lunar races and
find grilled zlorch and home-fried sneedams for forty people?

     I have put in a video to the local Never-Fail outlet,
but they have not sent a replacement as they said they would.

     Would you kindly see that this matter is attended to
without further delay.  I await a video reply at your earliest
possible convenience.

Yours truly,

Grant James

Grant James
```

Long Business Letters

Most business letters will be only one page, like the examples given. If you need more pages to complete your message, identify each page of the letter. The first page will look like the examples above, minus the closing. The following pages should give the name of the person or company to whom the letter is addressed, the page number, and the date, single-spaced in the upper left-hand corner. The bottom of each page (including the first) should indicate there are pages to follow by the word "continues" in the lower righthand corner.

Sage Productions
Page 2
1986 – 11 – 29

continues

When you think you have completed writing a business letter, apply this final test for quality:

"Have I provided all the necessary information in a clear, well-organized, and polite manner in order to receive a serious and prompt reply?"

Note: Make a copy of every business letter you write (with either carbon paper or a copying machine). This is especially useful with letters of complaint where it may be necessary to establish the date of the original claim. Never send your only copy of a letter.

Forms of Address

The way in which you handle the name, address, and salutation in a business letter is important. Here are some points to watch:

- The name and address of the recipient should be exactly the same both inside the letter and on the envelope. (See also *Envelopes and Folding*, *page 134*.)

- The name of the person and/or company should be complete and in the proper form. Include the person's surname, given name or initials, and title: Mr., Mrs., Miss, Ms., Dr., and so on. After the person's name, give his or her position in the company, if known — Sales Manager, Warehouse Supervisor, and so on.

- All names should be spelled correctly. It is irritating to have one's name misspelled.

- The address should be as complete as possible. An incompletely addressed letter may never reach its destination.

- In the salutation, use the person's title and surname only. Do not include the given name or initials.

Here is a table to aid you in choosing the correct form of address for special situations:

Addressee	Address	Salutation
Member of the House of Commons	Mr. Arthur Sinclair, M.P.	Dear Sir (Madam):
Member of a Provincial Government	Ms. Rita Larsen, M.L.A. (M.N.A. for Quebec; M.P.P. for Ontario)	Dear Madam (Sir):
Mayor of a City or Town	Her Worship Mayor Franz or Her Worship the Mayor of St. John's	Dear Madam (Mr.) Mayor: or Dear Madam (Sir):
Judge of a County or District Court	Her Honour Judge DeLeon	Dear Judge DeLeon:
Minister of Religion	The Reverend A. F. Gorden	Reverend Sir (Madam): or Dear Mr. (Mrs./Miss/Ms./ Dr.) Gorden:
Priest	The Reverend Father Hall	Reverend Sir: or Dear Father Hall:
Rabbi	Rabbi J. S. Greene	Dear Rabbi Greene: or Dear Sir:

Physician	Dr. Margaret Robinson or Margaret Robinson, M.D. (Never use both Dr. and M.D.)	Dear Dr. Robinson:
Dentist	Dr. William McBride or William McBride, D.D.S. (Never use both Dr. and D.D.S.)	Dear Dr. McBride:

LETTERS SEEKING EMPLOYMENT

Whether it relates to a summer, part-time, or full-time job, a letter to a potential employer should be designed to make a *good impression*. Your letter will be judged on the basis of

- what you say
- how you say it
- whether or not you have used the correct letter format
- whether or not you have followed all the rules of grammar, spelling, punctuation, and neatness

Application

Purpose:	to apply and be favourably considered for a job advertised in the newspaper
Audience:	Mrs. S. Hinman, Personnel Manager
Statement of Purpose:	I am writing a formal letter of application to Mrs. Hinman in the hope of being favourably considered for a job advertised in the newspaper.

The pattern followed in the letter of application on the following page can be applied to almost any person or situation. Each paragraph performs a specific function.

Paragraph 1
identifies the purpose of the letter and the specific job for which application is being made.

Paragraphs 2, 3
calls attention to the writer's qualifications, highlighting areas that are pertinent to the specific job.

calls attention to the fact that a résumé (and any other supplementary information) is enclosed.

Paragraph 4
expresses enthusiasm for the job and the company and a desire to be granted an interview.

- The writer says she will make a follow-up call. This point shows initiative and enthusiasm. It is better than simply saying, "I will look forward to hearing from you."
- Letters of application should not exceed one page if at all possible.

(See also *Interviews, page 146*.)

817 Flatt Street
Edmonton, Alberta
T5K 4S2

1988-04-21

Mrs. S. Hinman
Personnel Manager
United Products Corporation
129 Jasper Avenue
Edmonton, Alberta
T6L 5R3

Dear Mrs. Hinman:

I am writing to apply for the position of receptionist in your
Sales Division at United Products Corporation as advertised
in the Edmonton Journal today.

I will graduate from St. Justin Senior High School in June.
Over the last four years, I have taken a secretarial course
which included bookkeeping, typing, shorthand, academic subjects,
and studies in advertising and sales techniques. I have achieved
a B+ average in these subjects.

As you will note in my resume, which is enclosed, I have worked
part-time during the summer months and after school in the
office of Gregg Realty since the beginning of my high school
career. I began as a file clerk, but my duties were gradually
expanded to include typing and, last summer, reception. This
experience has given me an opportunity to apply my school
training to a business setting and to familiarize myself with
the responsibilities of office and sales personnel. I plan to
take night classes in psychology and personal dynamics next fall
and winter.

I would very much like to meet with you to learn more about the
position at United Products and to discuss my qualifications.
I will call you early next week to learn when it would be
convenient for you to see me.

Yours sincerely,

Jane Chung.

(Miss) Jane Chung

enclosure

Follow-Up

Purpose:	to follow up on my job interview
Audience:	Mrs. Hinman, Personnel Manager
Statement of Purpose:	I am writing a formal, brief letter as a follow-up to the job interview I had with Mrs. Hinman.

The purpose of this type of letter is to keep your name fresh in the potential employer's mind. Such a letter shows courtesy, initiative, and persistence.

```
817 Flatt Street
Edmonton, Alberta
T5K 4S2

1988-05-04


Mrs. S. Hinman
Personnel Manager
United Products Corporation
129 Jasper Avenue
Edmonton, Alberta
T6L 5R3

Dear Mrs. Hinman:

Thank you for the time and consideration you gave me in
the interview yesterday afternoon.  I appreciated the
opportunity to meet with you and to learn more about the
receptionist position available at United Products
Corporation.

I was particularly interested to learn that the position
would offer the possibility of moving into sales at a
later date.  As I mentioned in our discussion, I have
always enjoyed meeting people, and my experience with
Gregg Realty has aroused in me a strong interest in the
selling field.

I feel that I can make a positive contribution to United
Products and would very much like the opportunity to do
so.  Again, I thank you for your consideration.  I look
forward to hearing from you.

Yours sincerely,


Jane Chung.

Jane Chung
```

The pattern for such a letter is easy to follow:

Paragraph 1

expresses thanks for consideration given in a *very* recent interview and mentions the job in question specifically.

Paragraph 2

notes something specific you learned in the interview and tells why this piece of information was interesting and exciting to you.

reinforces that you are well qualified for the job.

Paragraph 3

restates your enthusiasm for the job and the company.

Résumé

Your résumé is your public biography, arranged by category and presented in point form. To make a good résumé, begin by writing a rough draft of the information you will include. Here are the categories to cover, usually in this order:

1. **Personal Data:**
   Your name, address, phone number, and date of birth are essential.

2. **Education:**
   Give the name of the school you are now attending and list any courses you are taking or have taken that relate directly to the kind of job you are seeking. Be sure to call attention to any outstanding scholastic achievement.

3. **Work Experience:**
   This should be a listing of any jobs you have held, including summer jobs, part-time jobs, and volunteer work. Begin with your most recent job and work back, listing the name of each company and your superior, the dates of your employment with that firm, and a *brief* description of your duties.

4. **Extracurricular Activities and Interests:**
   This section can contain a variety of things, but it should be brief. List any special activities and events you have participated in, talents or skills, and hobbies or interests. This kind of information can be given to show that you have a sense of responsibility, a talent for leadership, or a well-rounded personality, all of which are desirable to most employers.

5. **References:**
   List two or three references, which you have permission to give, providing the name, position, address, and phone number of each person you are suggesting. *Or* simply state, "References will be furnished upon request." (See also *References, page 134.*)

6. **Photograph:**
   A personal photograph is optional. It should be a small head-and-shoulders portrait, mounted in the upper right-hand corner of the résumé.

Try to get the information on a single sheet but use two if the résumé is going to look cramped.

Always send a résumé with a covering letter, however brief, even if you have already made a verbal application in person or by telephone.

Here is an example of a well-done résumé:

```
JANE CHUNG
817 Flatt Street
Edmonton, Alberta T5K 4S2
TELEPHONE:        (403) 428-5121

DATE OF BIRTH:  1970-09-14
```

EDUCATION:

- Will graduate from St. Justin Senior High School, Edmonton, Alberta T2K 1B4 in June 1988.

- Completed a four-year business course and attained a typing speed of 50 wpm, a shorthand speed of 120 wpm, and a working knowledge of intermediate bookkeeping. Specialized in advertising and sales technique.

- Achieved a B+ average.

- Participated in a seminar, "Opening the Door to Selling", sponsored by the Edmonton Businessmen's Association.

EXPERIENCE:

September 1986 to present
Gregg Realty
24 Spruce Avenue
Edmonton, Alberta T2B 3K3
(403) 816-2143
Sales Manager: Mr. E. Fisher

Part-time clerk/typist
Duties included filing, typing sales letters and advertisements and reception.

July to August 1986
Sunnyfield Nursing Home
43 Reishton Avenue
Edmonton, Alberta T2K 2N7
(403) 802-1279
Supervisor: Ms. P. Wallach

Volunteer reader
3 afternoons a week, read aloud to blind patients for 2 hours. Also fetched and returned library books for sighted patients.

EXTRACURRICULAR ACTIVITIES:

- Member of Broad Street United Church Choir, 768 Poplar Avenue, Edmonton, Alberta T2K 2N7.

- Member of Y-Teen at St. Justin Senior High during my last three years. Book sale coordinator Christmas 1986 and 1987.

- Spring 1988, Coordinator of ticket sales for St. Justin's Spring Concert, which sold out all but one of six performances.

REFERENCES:

- Ms. P. Wallach, Supervisor, Sunnyfield Nursing Home, 43 Reishton Avenue, Edmonton, Alberta T2K 2N7, (403) 802-1279

- Mr. E. Fisher, Gregg Realty, 24 Spruce Avenue, Edmonton, Alberta T2B 3K3, (403) 816-2143

References Here are the points to consider when making a list of references:

- Choose people who know you well enough to speak knowledgeably and fairly about you.
- Try to select people who can comment favourably on your work-related abilities, especially former employers.
- After former employers, consider teachers, school staff, neighbours, and friends' parents — in that order — as potential references. Do not give your parents, relatives, or friends as references unless you have a very special reason for doing so (for example, if you worked directly for your uncle for the last three summers).
- Never give anyone as a reference unless you have received clear and direct permission to do so. You may obtain this permission either in person or by a formal business letter.

Checklist for Seeking Employment

Have I:

1. Written a complete résumé and made a sufficient number of copies of it?
2. Obtained permission to use the names of two or three people as references?
3. Written a letter of application?
4. Prepared to answer questions of a potential employer in an interview? (See also *Interviews, page 146.*)
5. Written a follow-up letter for each interview granted to me?

ENVELOPES AND FOLDING

- Envelopes for friendly letters may vary in size, but for business letters the correct size is 24.0 cm × 10.5 cm ($9^{1}/_{2}''$ × $4^{1}/_{8}''$).
- Envelopes should always include your return address as well as the *complete* address of the person to whom you are writing.
- Here is how a correctly addressed envelope should look:

Your Address
571 Grover Street
St. John's, Newfoundland
A4E 3S9

CANADA A — Stamp

Recipient's name and address; start a little above and to the left of centre
Ms. Joni Gerrard
14 Fraser Drive
Vancouver, British Columbia
V8Z 7A5

Minimum 3.5 cm space

- Friendly letters should have as few folds as possible. Such letters are sometimes written on prefolded cards.

- Business letters and letters seeking employment are written on white 21.5 cm × 28.0 cm (8½″ × 11″) paper, and they are always folded in thirds. Remember to include any extra material, such as a résumé.

- The correct postal code is important on *all* envelopes. Postal codes can be found in the postal code directory at any postal station. The postal code should be placed on a line by itself, at the bottom of the address.

- Before mailing your letter, double-check the envelope. Is the address complete and correct? Have you remembered to put on a stamp?

Friendly Letter

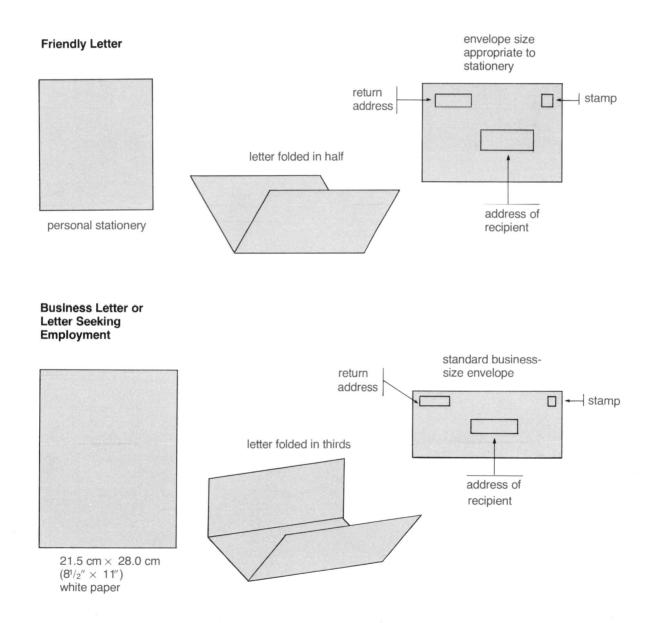

personal stationery

letter folded in half

envelope size appropriate to stationery

return address

stamp

address of recipient

Business Letter or Letter Seeking Employment

21.5 cm × 28.0 cm (8½″ × 11″) white paper

letter folded in thirds

standard business-size envelope

return address

stamp

address of recipient

CHECKLIST FOR LETTER WRITING

Have I:

1. Composed my message with my purpose and audience clearly in mind?

2. Written neatly in ink or typed on clean paper (white for business or employment letters)?

3. Followed the formats given in this section for the three different kinds of letters?

4. Followed all the rules of spelling, grammar, and punctuation?

5. Made a neat, legible, and correct envelope?

6. Written a letter I would be pleased to receive?

Test yourself:

There are nine errors or omissions in the following business letter. What are they? How would you correct them? (Hint: None of the errors are in grammar or spelling.)

```
      1985-03-29


      Mrs. Eleanor Winters
      Hotel St. John's
      102-108 Kenmount Road
      St. John's, Newfoundland

      Dear Mrs. Winters,

      My biology class is currently planning a summer trip to
      St. John's and the surrounding area.  We will be studying
      marine life.  Your hotel was recommended to us by my
      neighbour, who stayed there last September.

      I am writing on behalf of my class to see if you will
      have rooms available in July.  Is a group rate offered?
      If so, what is the group rate?

      Please send me all the information you have available
      on Hotel St. John's.  We will be finalizing our plans
      soon.

      Thank you for your trouble.  I look forward to hearing
      from you.

      Thank you:
```

CHAPTER 7
Listening and Speaking

LISTENING AND SPEAKING

Speaking in public is rarely easy, but with
enough experience and the right techniques, you
may discover that speaking can be exciting and
can be a learning experience. This Chapter offers
some tips for improving both your speaking and
listening skills.

CONTENTS

EFFECTIVE LISTENING

Listening is so much a part of everyday life that we may not think of it as a skill. But if it is well developed, listening is a valuable asset — in school and in everyday life.

Effective listening means being an *active* listener. The skilled listener is more than a passive observer. He or she uses a number of techniques to get as much as possible out of the listening experience.

Three Steps to Active Listening

Three simple steps will help you to be a good listener in any situation.

STEP 1: Be prepared to listen.

The key to listening is *concentration*. Start by tuning out all distractions. Make sure you are comfortable; look directly at the speaker as much as possible.

The person who is talking is usually influenced by how you listen. If you are attentive, you help the speaker to say clearly what she or he has in mind. Looking at the speaker will also help you pick up the more subtle messages conveyed by body language.

STEP 2: Decide the purpose of listening for each occasion.

Here are a few of the reasons why you might listen to another person or to a group of people:

- to gather information (example: a science lecture)
- to be mentally stimulated or challenged (example: a guest speaker)
- to get help in forming an opinion (example: a political debate)
- to be inspired (example: a religious leader)
- to broaden your understanding (example: a foreign visitor)
- to develop closeness (example: a friend)

When you think about *why* you are listening, you help yourself get more meaning from the listening experience.

STEP 3: Plan how you will fulfil your purpose for listening.

This step in the listening process requires you to *act* upon the decision made in Step 2. Here are some examples of how to do that:

Decision Made in Step 2	Action in Step 3
(a) I am listening to gather information.	• Bring paper and pencils to take notes. • Write down main ideas *only*. • Make note of any questions that occur to you. • Review or transcribe your notes *soon* after the event to clear up misunderstandings early.

(b) I am listening to gain help in forming an opinion.

- Make note of main ideas.
- Consider the overall meaning of what is said.
- Critically analyse the validity of each point.
- Be prepared to ask questions.

(c) I am listening to develop closeness with a friend.

- Try to understand the other person's needs, personality, and point of view. Relate them to your own past experience.
- Ask questions that show interest in and understanding of the other person.

Barriers to Listening

Being an effective listener also means not letting barriers interfere with your listening.

- Try to block out all distractions.
- Listen for the main ideas and note the details later.
- Avoid getting emotionally upset and presenting arguments before the speaker is finished.
- Evaluate *what* is said, not *how* it is said. Avoid criticizing the speaker's personality or manner of presentation.

Making Notes in Lectures or Discussions

It is sometimes useful to make notes on what you are listening to, especially in a classroom. Some people have trouble taking notes because they try to write down *everything* a speaker says. Three key points are worth remembering.

- It is most effective to write down the *main ideas* of a lecture or discussion. Usually a lecture is organized so that the main points stand out clearly.
- Try to spend more time listening than writing. Think about what you hear *before* you write it down. Learn to distinguish between main points and minor details.
- Ask yourself *questions* about the main ideas presented. Write them down so you can ask the speaker to answer them. (See also *Making Notes, page 11*.)

As a general guideline:

- Be prepared to listen.
- Decide why you are listening.
- Make plans so that you can benefit the most from listening.

EFFECTIVE SPEAKING

Here are four steps that will help you to be a success in public speaking:

STEP 1: Be prepared.

This step is designed to help you to use your time efficiently as you work through the next three steps.

(a) Begin by learning all you can about the *context* in which you will speak. Ask yourself:

- Is it a debate? A prepared speech by me alone? A panel discussion? A meeting?

- Will I be expected to ask questions? Answer questions?

- Will the room in which I speak be too large for posters or illustrations to be used? Will there be a microphone — and if so, can I practise with it in advance?

- Will there be a fixed time limit for my comments or presentation?

(b) Next, learn all you can about your *topic*.

- If you are to give a speech, anticipate possible questions and plan how you will answer.

- If you are to be the chairperson of a discussion, talk with each of the participants and learn what kinds of information each will have to offer and what role each is likely to play.

- If you are participating in a debate, coordinate your presentation with your partner's and anticipate the arguments of the opposing side.

STEP 2 and STEP 3: Know your purpose and your audience.

Once you know about the context in which you will be speaking and about the topic of the discussion, decide on your *purpose* (so you will know what to say) and your *audience* (so you will know how to say it). Here are some examples:

Purpose	What to Say
(a) To present a science project	• Describe project plan and format. • Provide facts. • Give findings. • Explain conclusions.
(b) To open a meeting	• Welcome the group. • List topics to be discussed. • Follow any club procedures.
(c) To deliver a speech to persuade school officials	• State a position with facts. • Give arguments to support your position. • Address any contrary opinions openly. • Restate your position firmly.

Audience	How to Say It
(a) Your own science class	• Draw upon information known to the class as a whole. • Highlight anything not familiar to the class. • Be well organized, concise, and relaxed.
(b) Members of your photography club	• Be relaxed and casual; you are among friends. • Know what you are going to say, but remember it is an informal meeting; the group has gathered by choice and for recreation. • Feel free to use slang, but don't joke around so much that nothing is accomplished.
(c) School officials and members of the community	• Be formal, concise, and well prepared. • Be highly respectful of your audience but not too modest or apologetic. • Stick rigorously to the topic.

STEP 4: Practise delivery

A speaker must immediately get the attention of his or her audience and then hold this attention during the rest of the speech. The speaker's voice and body language are important factors that influence the reaction of the audience. Practise the speech before you deliver it to an audience. Here are some questions to use as guidelines while practising delivery:

• Am I speaking loudly and distinctly enough to be heard by *everyone* in the room?

• Am I speaking at a reasonable *pace* — slowly enough for each word to be clear, quickly enough to sound natural?

• Am I making *eye contact* with the people in the audience?

• Am I standing straight but *not rigid*? Are my gestures natural and smooth?

• Am I changing the *tone of my voice* to make new points or stress important statements?

• Do I *pause* occasionally to give my listeners time to digest an important point or to mark a thought break between topics?

• Am I saying "um" or "er" too frequently?

- Can I use my *note cards* as quick reminders without having to stop and read to myself?

- Is my presentation *natural and appropriate* to my purpose and my audience?

The best way to practise is with an audience. If you cannot enlist friends or family members to comment on your delivery, be your own audience and practise before a mirror. Be conscious of any mannerisms that may annoy an audience, such as continually clearing your throat or chopping the air with your hand. Remember, too, that each time you speak up in a group, you are getting practice in public speaking; the more you do it, the easier it becomes.

GROUP DISCUSSIONS

A good group discussion involves a small enough number of people so that everyone has an opportunity to participate. Group discussions provide an excellent environment

- for sharing information
- for answering complex questions
- for solving problems

Different types of group discussions are conducted in different ways. Here are some guidelines.

Brainstorming

When a group of people gather for the purpose of solving a single, specific problem, they are *brainstorming*. This same kind of gathering is also often called a problem-solving session. Here is how to brainstorm:

1. Have a chairperson introduce the topic and state the problem.

2. If the group is large, consider breaking off into smaller groups and then reassembling when each group has a specific proposal to make. This approach can save time and give each person a chance to express his or her views.

3. Encourage each member to present as many ideas as possible, no matter how impractical they may seem. One person's idea will stimulate the creativity of another.

4. Listen carefully to each person's point of view and strive to be objective.

5. Strive for cooperation within the group; avoid making remarks that are negative or too critical.

6. Narrow down the number of possible solutions and then analyse each proposal in detail. (If you have broken into smaller groups, this is the time to reassemble. A leader from each group should report on what the group has decided.)

As a general guideline:

- Encourage full participation by all the members of the group and do not react in a negative manner to suggestions.

- Listen objectively to each idea presented.
- Stick to the topic being discussed.

Committees

A committee is made up of a small group of people who have been asked to work on behalf of a larger group. A committee may be formed

- to solve a problem (see also *Brainstorming, previous section*.)
- to gather information
- to monitor an ongoing situation
- to initiate and carry out a specific task (such as ticket-selling)

Each time a committee meets, there is a group discussion. This discussion will usually be most productive if the committee has a chairperson and if each member of the committee has a specific area on which to report. (See also *Role of the Chairperson, page 146*.)

As a general guideline:

- Begin by defining the purpose of the discussion.
- Stay on the subject at hand.
- Give each person a chance to participate.
- Allow the chairperson to lead the group to a workable plan or solution.

Panels

A panel is made up of three to seven people who are knowledgeable about a specific topic. In a panel discussion, the panellists sit before an audience and talk among themselves in voices loud enough to be heard by the audience. The audience has the opportunity to hear differing points of view on a topic.

Most panel discussions have a chairperson or moderator. Many such discussions allow for a question period with audience participation.

As a general guideline:

- Be well informed about the topic to be discussed.
- Speak loudly enough to be heard by the audience.
- Be respectful of the other panel members' opinions and do not interrupt.
- Listen attentively to each speaker and separate fact from opinion.
- Be prepared to ask questions of the panel members.

Symposiums

A symposium is a gathering of well-informed individuals, each of whom is prepared to give a formal presentation on a specific aspect of the subject of the symposium. These presentations are usually given before an audience. Unlike a panel discussion, a symposium does not necessarily involve discussion among the members of the group before the audience.

A symposium usually has a chairperson or moderator who introduces each participant and explains his or her area of expertise. Most symposiums allow for a question period following each formal presentation.

As a general guideline:

- Be fully prepared to speak in depth on the subject assigned to you.
- Be generally informed about the topics to be covered by other members of the symposium so that you can ask or respond to questions.
- Listen attentively to each speaker, with a view toward asking questions.
- Try to compare and evaluate differing points of view among the participants. (See also *Speeches, page 148.*)

Forums

A forum is a group discussion in which everyone has an opportunity to express views or ask questions. Usually one topic is designated for review. Often a panel will provide information or opinions in response to questions from the audience.

A forum must have a chairperson or moderator to call upon members of the audience and to direct questions to the appropriate panel members.

As a general guideline:

- Stick to the topic being discussed.
- Listen carefully to each person who speaks.
- Wait to be recognized by the chairperson before you speak.

Formal Meetings

A meeting is usually a regular gathering of people who belong to a club or organization. A meeting can be either *formal* or *informal*.

A *formal meeting* is conducted by a chairperson according to the rules of parliamentary procedure. It follows a specific plan (prepared and distributed in advance by the chairperson) called an *agenda*. (See also *Committees, p. 143.*) A formal meeting usually follows this pattern:

1. Call to order by the chairperson
2. Reading or distribution of the minutes of the previous meeting (The *minutes* are the official record of the meeting and are kept by the secretary.)
3. Reports of various committees
4. Unfinished business from previous meetings
5. New business
6. Announcements
7. Adjournment by the chairperson

All remarks in a formal meeting are addressed to the chairperson.

Decisions in a formal meeting are made by *motions* followed by *voting*. A motion is a formal suggestion put before the group for consideration, such as, "I move that we invite a member of parliament to speak at our next meeting."

Here is the process by which a motion leads to a decision by the group.

1. The person making the motion begins his or her statement by saying, "I move that . . ."

2. A motion requires a "seconder", a person who agrees that this motion is a good idea. The seconder says, "I second the motion."

3. A discussion of the motion follows. Anyone wishing to speak raises his or her hand to address the chairperson.

4. When discussion seems near an end, the chairperson will ask, "Is there any further discussion?" If not, voting follows. Generally, motions are voted on by a show of hands. The chairperson votes only if there is a tie.

Note: For further information on parliamentary procedure as it is practised in formal meetings, see *Robert's Rules of Order*. Most libraries carry this book.

As a general guideline:

- Everyone must understand in advance the system to be used for conducting the meeting.

- Everyone must accept a responsibility to contribute and to listen to the contributions of others.

- Everyone should strive to stick to the topic at hand and to respect the direction of the chairperson.

Informal Debates

The word *debate* means "a discussion of the arguments for and against something". Any two people can have a debate. This section will show how to engage in an *informal* debate, designed to involve everyone present.

Note: The rules for formal debates can be found in several books in the library.

Here is a five-stage plan for an informal classroom debate:

1. **Decision on a Topic:** The statement of a topic is called a *resolution*. This resolution should be phrased in the form of a *simple statement*, preceded by the words "Resolved that:". For example,

> "Resolved that: Shakespeare's *Hamlet* is not relevant to today's youth."

A good debate topic is very specific. Notice that the example names a single play by Shakespeare, instead of saying, "Shakespeare is not relevant . . ."

2. **Presentation of Opposing Views:** Choose four members of the class to present the arguments for the debate. These people will have to do research and prepare their statements before the class meets to debate.

Two people will be the *affirmative*. That is, they agree with the statement made in the resolution. Two people will be the *negative*. That is, they disagree with the statement made in the resolution.

The four people alternate, each presenting five-minute speeches. The other members of the class should listen carefully and make notes of the speakers' opinions during this time. Class members should also make notes of their own thoughts on the topic.

3. **Refuting:** Each member of the debating team is allowed a few minutes in which to try to refute, or prove to be incorrect, the arguments put forward by the opposing side.

4. **Question Period:** This is a ten-minute period in which the members of the class may direct questions to the four debaters. A chairperson should call on those who wish to ask questions.

5. **The Vote:** At the end of the question period, the chairperson should ask for a vote by a show of hands to decide which side has won the debate.

As a general guideline:

- If you are one of the four debaters, be fully prepared. Rely on facts and sound reasoning to support your point of view. Anticipate the arguments likely to be presented by the opposing side. Anticipate the questions from the audience.

- If you are in the audience, listen with an open mind. Be objective. Judge the two opposing views on the strength of the arguments, not on personalities. Take notes. Prepare your questions.

- All participants must stick to the topic and respect the time limitations.

Role of the Chairperson

Group discussions are usually more productive if there is a chairperson. This person

- prepares and distributes an agenda or outline in advance (See also *Meetings, page 144*.)

- makes an opening statement, setting forth the purpose of the discussion

- gives each person a chance to participate

- ensures that participants stick to the subject

- encourages participants to show courtesy and respect for others

- provides a summary at the end of the discussion or at any time during the discussion when a review would be productive

---

As a general guideline:

- See that the discussion is clear, productive, and fair.

INTERVIEWS

An interview is often an effective method of obtaining information. You may want to interview people when you are preparing reports or projects for school, and you will probably be interviewed when you apply for a job. Here are some guidelines for each case.

When you are the interviewer. . .

1. Establish a plan.

- Decide who is the best person to ask about the subject in which you are interested.

- Write or call that person to arrange for the interview. State why you would like to conduct the interview and make an appointment to meet the person at his or her convenience.

- Prepare a list of questions. Arrange them in a logical order. Phrase questions so that the person will give a full answer, not simply yes or no. Be clear and specific about what you want to know.

- Bring a clipboard or a hard-backed notebook, so that you can take notes without the aid of a desk. Bring enough paper and pencils, so that you do not have to impose on the person you are interviewing.

2. Conduct the interview efficiently.

- Arrive on time and be friendly and courteous.

- Greet the person and restate the reason for the interview.

- Ask questions one at a time. Listen carefully and take brief notes. If a response is interesting or surprising, ask the person to elaborate.

- If you would like to use a quotation later on, make sure you copy down each word exactly. Read the statement back to the person and ask permission to use it as a direct quotation.

- Manage your time carefully. For example, if you have thirty minutes and ten questions, do not spend fifteen minutes on the first two questions. Ask important questions first.

- Thank the person for his or her time and consideration.

3. Follow up immediately.

- Write a brief letter of thanks. (See also *Business Letters, page 123*.)

- Review your notes. Expand on what you have written while the interview is fresh in your mind. Write down thoughts and impressions. Draw conclusions.

- If you *must* phone the interview subject to clarify a point, do so as soon as possible. Phone only once.

When you are being interviewed for a job. . .

1. Plan carefully in advance.

- Anticipate the interviewer's questions and try to plan responses. The following are some typical *general* questions that *might* be asked.
    a) Why did you choose this particular field?
    b) What personal characteristics do you feel are necessary in your chosen field?
    c) Do you prefer working with other people or by yourself?
    d) How do you respond to criticism?
    e) What are your future educational plans?
    f) Are you willing to work overtime when necessary?
    g) What are your major strengths and weaknesses? What aspect of yourself would you like to improve?

- Be prepared to provide information about yourself. Bring anything you might need to take a test or to demonstrate your aptitude for the job for which you have applied.

- Make sure that you know exactly how to get to the place of the interview and how long it will take to get there.

2. Make a good impression.

- Be on time.

- Be courteous and respectful but not excessively modest or shy.

- Listen carefully to each question and answer it directly and concisely. Speak clearly and do not use slang or informal language.

- Try to emphasize your strong points.

- Ask questions about the job and the company. Show enthusiasm and interest, but do not try to monopolize the interview.

- Thank the person for his or her time and consideration. Try to learn when the decision about the job will be made and how you will be informed of the decision.

3. Follow up immediately.

- Write a follow-up letter of thanks. (*See also Letters of Employment, page 129.*)

SPEECHES

A speech is a spoken essay. Like an essay, it can be used to inform, explain, entertain, persuade, impress, or any combination of these.

A good speech is carefully planned, written, and practised in advance.

Two sections in this book will help you to prepare the best speech for any occasion:

First, follow the eight steps of the writing process. (See *The Writing Process, page 16*.) These steps will guide you in planning, preparing, and refining what you will say. At Step 8, make up small 7 cm × 13 cm (3″ × 5″) notecards that you can refer to for reminders during the speech. Write brief notes on each card so that you can read them quickly. They are *reminders*. Here is a sample note card/reminder for a speaker:

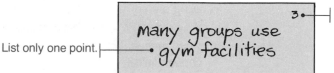

The second section in this book that will help in preparing a speech is *Effective Speaking, page 140*. Pay special attention to Step 4, Practise Delivery. Good delivery is inseparable from a good speech.

Following are some special occasions that may require a speech.

Announcements

An announcement is a short statement designed to give information and arouse interest. It should be complete and accurate. Make sure that you have *all* of the information that you will need before you give the announcement. An announcement should include some or all of the following, depending on the subject:

- the name of the group sponsoring the event
- the nature of the event
- the date, time, and place of the event
- the price of tickets and where to buy them
- the purpose of the event
- how the listener or reader can respond if the announcement is not about ticket sales or an event

Here is a sample announcement:

> The Girls' Athletic League is sponsoring a dance. It will be held next Friday, October 31, at 8 p.m. in the school gymnasium. Come and have a good time. Since Friday will be Halloween, the dance will be a costume party; prizes will be given for the best costumes. Tickets are $2 each and are on sale at the student council office. Remember, the dance is on Friday, October 31, at 8 p.m. in the gym. Proceeds will be used for new uniforms for the girls' basketball team.

Note: The key information (date, time, and place) has been repeated for emphasis.

Introducing a Guest Speaker

An introduction should be brief and interesting. It should not take longer than a minute or two. Your most important job is to tell the audience *who* is speaking and *why* he or she is speaking. The introduction should include a sketch of the speaker's life and professional activities as they relate to the speech topic. Brief mention can also be made of particular talents or experiences of the speaker that are unusual or will be of interest to the audience.

Here are some points to keep in mind when you introduce a speaker:

- Include the speaker's name and why he or she has been invited to speak.
- Include a few complimentary sentences expressing the audience's enthusiasm to hear the speaker.
- Turn to the speaker and invite him or her to the podium by repeating the speaker's name so that it is clearly heard by the audience.

It is always best to speak or correspond with a person you will be asked to introduce prior to the event. If the person being introduced has an opportunity to read or approve your remarks in advance, you will be saved the embarrassment of making an inaccurate or inappropriate introduction.

Here is a sample introduction:

> Ladies and gentlemen, I have the honour to introduce to you the main speaker of the evening, Superman, who will speak to us on the subject, "Growing Up as a Boy of Steel". Most of us know of Superman's leaping tall buildings at a single bound and being more powerful than a locomotive. He is also well known as a crimefighter and a staunch defender of life, liberty, and the pursuit of happiness. He has flown to us today from the city of Metropolis to speak on his early life, and I am sure that we will be thrilled to hear how many footballs he kicked beyond the school goalposts and how he finished his afternoon chores in seconds flat. You'll agree, I'm sure, that we have in store a really "super" speech. And now it gives me great pleasure to call upon Superman.

Presenting an Award

A speech presenting an award should be brief, specific, and spirited. Mention who is giving the award but keep the emphasis on the person receiving it. Try to include some experience or anecdote about the recipient.

Here is a simple format for an award speech:

- Tell the audience what you are going to present and to whom.
- Explain the reason for the award.
- Make the presentation.

A sample presentation speech might sound like this:

> Fellow club members, we are here tonight to honour our retiring president, Alice Beck, and present her with a silver gavel for her expert leadership during the past year. I know we all recall with admiration her efforts to establish a school liaison committee and her arranging scholarships for needy students. I especially remember a snowy February day when we had to change taxis three times in rush-hour traffic in order to get to an important meeting. The going was rough, but Alice was always equal to the struggle. And now, Alice, it gives me great pleasure to present you with this silver gavel.

Accepting an Award

An acceptance speech should be as brief and as warm as the presentation speech that preceded it. Here are some points to keep in mind:

- Begin by saying, "Thank you."
- Express appreciation to the organization that has made the award possible and to the organization actually granting the award, if they are different.
- Mention and give credit to the people who have helped you achieve the award.
- Be brief and sincere. Close by repeating, "Thank you."

An acceptance speech for the presentation of the silver gavel might sound like this:

> Thank you for the marvellous gift you have given me. It will always be a memento of the year I've spent as president of the PTA. And thank you for your support. Without it, I'd never have been able to raise that scholarship money. I'd especially like to thank the committee members who wrote letters, made phone calls, and visited corporations around the city. I know that the scholarship money will be put to good use, giving our children the education they need to be tomorrow's leaders. Again, thank you for helping me work toward that goal and for remembering me so kindly with this token of your appreciation.

Toasts

A toast is a statement of respect or affection for a person or persons. Those who are gathered together for an occasion, such as a wedding or an award presentation, may be asked to drink to the health of the newly married couple or to the recipient of the award. As with most speeches, the person who makes the toast should be brief and sincere. Here are some points to keep in mind:

- Explain the purpose of the toast.
- Explain briefly why the person or persons deserve the honour of the toast. A personal note is usually a good idea.
- Formally call for everyone present to drink to the health of those who are to be honoured.

Here is a sample wedding toast:

> Ladies and gentlemen, we are here to celebrate the wedding of Jim Green and Mary Brown. I would like to propose a toast to the happy couple, whom I've known almost all my life. The three of us were friends in school together, and I remember that even at school dances they only had eyes for each other. I'm sure that they will have a joyful life together. I call on you all to rise and drink to the health of the newlyweds.

A reply to a toast should be very brief and to the point. All that is required is a statement of thanks for the kindness, best wishes, and thoughtfulness of the presenter of the toast and those who have joined in the toast.

As a general guideline:

- Thoroughly prepare what you will say *and* practise how you will say it.
- Stick to the time limits specified. Always be concise.
- Remember that a good speech is never *read*. It is *delivered* in a natural and conversational manner.

ILLUSTRATED TALKS AND DEMONSTRATIONS

Illustrated Talks

An illustrated talk involves the coordination of spoken and visual material. Visual materials may include posters, charts, graphs, and overhead projections. Here are some guidelines for giving an illustrated talk:

- Use illustrations only if they provide new information or present information in a way that cannot be done effectively with words alone.
- Use only illustrations that can be seen and understood easily by all the members of the audience.
- Practise how to use the illustrations, including how to point to them or to particular aspects of them, until you feel *completely comfortable* using the visual aids.
- Small illustrations may be placed on a table, in the order in which they will be used, and held up one by one. Larger illustrations may be hung on a wall or placed on an easel. Do not stand between the audience and the illustration. Use a pointer.

Sometimes audio effects, such as records or tapes, can be added, especially if the speaker wants to create a certain mood or feeling. This type of presentation is usually called a *multi-media presentation*.

Demonstrations

Demonstrations are very similar to illustrated talks. They are common in science, technical, and art classes. Here are some guidelines for giving a demonstration:

- Begin by explaining the overall purpose of the demonstration.
- Show the audience each of the articles you will use in the demonstration.
- At each step of the demonstration, make certain that everyone in the audience has a chance to see exactly what you are doing. When possible, carry a portion of the demonstration into the centre of the audience. This method involves the audience in the presentation.
- Practise in advance. You must be able to talk informatively and naturally at the same time.

As a general guideline:

- Prepare the spoken part of your presentation just as you would for any speech.
- Practise using your visual aids or doing your demonstration until you are fully comfortable using all "the props".
- Time your preparation *using your props*. It will be much longer than the spoken part of the presentation delivered alone.

CHECKLIST FOR PUBLIC SPEAKING

Do I:

- know what I am going to say?
- know what is appropriate for the occasion?
- know what is appropriate for the audience?
- know the aspects of good delivery?

Have I:

- prepared and brought all the materials I need (note cards, illustrations, and so on)?
- practised my delivery so that I feel comfortable with it?

Test yourself:

1. Imagine that you have been asked to take notes at a school assembly in the auditorium where a member of parliament will be speaking. You take several sheets of paper out of your binder and two pencils. What have you forgotten?

2. Good speakers often use note cards. Part of the reason they are good speakers is that they know *how* to use note cards. Name two things that you can do that will make you better at using note cards.

3. Imagine that you have been asked to give an oral report to your class on a science project you did at home. What will you tell your classmates *first*?

4. Imagine that you have an important speech to give and that you want some friends to listen to you practise and give you constructive criticism on your speaking style. You ask them to count the number of times you say "um" and "er". What else should they watch for?

5. Imagine that you have to interview a supermarket manager for a report you are doing in your business class. The manager has promised you a thirty-minute interview. Name at least two things you can do to make the most of that time.

ANSWERS TO TEST YOURSELF

CHAPTER 2: PARAGRAPHS AND ESSAYS

Formal vs. Informal (page 30)

1. a is formal because it follows all the traditional rules of writing and presentation.

2. b is informal because it contains contractions and because most formal writing is not first person (I).

3. c is formal. Words like "burst on" need not be used only in informal writing. In this sentence, they accurately and interestingly describe what happened.

Transitions (page 33)

1. our sun or it

2. their or astronomers'

3. Soon or Eventually or In time (time transitional expression)

4. firey patterns or celestial pictures (synonym transition)

Variety (page 35)

There are many ways to make the story told in the paragraph interesting. Here is one of them.

Frankenstein, one of the earliest and most famous horror story characters, first appeared in an 1818 novel by Mary Wollstonecraft Shelley. Long after his appearance over a century and a half ago, Shelley's monster began to inspire movie-makers. Interestingly, most of the movies made share one significant error: The monster has the wrong name. In the original novel, the monster's creator was called Frankenstein, but the creature itself had no name at all.

Figurative Language (page 36)

1. as deadly as arsenic is a simile.

2. contains no figurative language

3. these eight-legged vampires is a metaphor that draws on the belief that vampires suck blood.

CHAPTER 3: RESEARCH PAPERS

Research Papers (page 50)

1. periodicals (magazines and newspapers) and reference books

2. The book will be listed in

    a) the author file under "Christopher",

    b) the title file under (The) Illustrated History of Magic, and

    c) the subject file under "MAGIC."

    The quickest way to find the book is to use the title file. Milbourne Christopher may have written more than one book — that means extra cards to flip through — and there will be a great many cards to search through under "magic." There will be only one title card.

3. Canadian Periodical Index and Reader's Guide to Periodical Literature

4. The page number showing exactly where the quotation can be found is missing. The page number is important because if you use the information on the card in your paper, you must give the page number in your footnote.

5. Yes. You may have done a great deal of research but you probably have not made a scientific study on people's thoughts about Houdini or magic. The idea for this sentence has come from an expert. You must credit him in your footnotes or you will have plagiarized his work.

CHAPTER 4: PRESENTING WRITTEN WORK

Formats (page 64)

1. the name of the student who wrote the essay; the date; the class or assignment name

2. a) the book's title

    b) the name(s) of author(s) and/or editor(s)

    c) the publisher's name

    d) the place of publication

    e) the date of publication

    f) the page(s) where you found useful information

3. a) a pie graph — to show percentages

    b) a line graph — to show a trend

CHAPTER 5: CHECKING WRITTEN WORK

Sentence Fragments (page 66)

1. a, b, d, e,

2. Here are some ways to revise the fragments.

    a) Most cats easily scramble to the tops of tall trees.

    b) The lion, equipped with sharp teeth and powerful jaws, is not lightly called the king of the jungle.

    d) Unlike lions and tigers, leopards are inclined to attack humans if they are frightened.

    e) Although jaguars are carnivores, or meat eaters, many people are surprised to find that, in addition to small mammals, they also have been known to catch and eat small fish.

Run-ons (page 67)

1. a, c, d
2. Here are some examples of how the run-ons can be revised.
   a) Hockey originated in Canada in the 1870s; it quickly spread to the United States.
   c) The Stanley Cup was first awarded in 1893 for the Canadian amateur championship, and from 1912 to 1925 it was awarded to the winner of a competition between the champions of the Pacific Coast League and the Eastern League.
   d) Modern-day competition for the Stanley Cup occurs in the spring of each year between the best teams of the NHL in a succession of games called the play-offs. Interestingly, these games are the only ones in which overtime periods are used to break ties.

Misplaced Modifiers (page 68)

The underlined phrases were the misplaced modifiers.

1. One of the most popular spy heroes of all time, James Bond, was created by a British author named Ian Fleming, who wrote the Bond novels in the 1950s and early 1960s.
2. Many parents tried to keep their children from reading Ian Fleming's James Bond novels, which were full of sex and violence.
3. contains no misplaced modifier
4. Although Ian Fleming died in 1964, apparently leaving Bond without a "father", Hollywood has kept the Bond character alive with such movies as *From Russia With Love* and *Goldfinger*.

Dangling Modifiers (page 68)

The underlined phrases were the dangling modifiers.

1. Always quick to see through a Spectre plot, James Bond did not appear to let his high style of life interfere with business.
2. contains no dangling modifiers
3. Relying on his skill in oriental martial arts, James Bond instantly defeated most enemy agents.
4. The sports car sped out ahead in every car chase when Bond activated the special rocket engines.

Awkward Sentences (page 69)

Here are some ways to revise the sentences.

1. After several scandals were bitterly criticized by the opposition, the party in power called an election.
2. As the worst of the scandals concerned oil price negotiations, a subject of considerable interest to the public, the opposition had the support of the people.
3. Increasingly, resources, whether oil, water, or mineral, are high-powered issues in the political arena.

Parallelism (page 70)

1. Thebes, Memphis, Alexandria, and Gizeh were all important cities in ancient Egypt.
2. The Mediterranean Sea, the Red Sea, the Nile, and Lake Nasser are all bodies of water that are important to the economy of modern-day Egypt.

Subject-verb Agreement (page 72)

1. controls
2. realize ; originates
3. carries; remain
4. buys; does

Verb Tense (page 73)

1. mixed tenses; write either needed/were or need/are
2. auxiliary verb missing; write I am jogging
3. wrong tense, use past perfect; write I had already jogged

Using Pronouns (page 76)

1. a) their is incorrect; the antecedent of their is "Charles Panati", which is singular.
   b) they is confusing; is the antecedent of they "teeth" (meaning "teeth are eventually painful") or "our mouths" (meaning "our mouths are eventually painful")? The reader has no way of knowing.
   c) who is incorrect; the antecedent of who is tooth decay, but who can only be used to replace a person or animal, not a thing like tooth decay.
   d) they is incorrect; the antecedent of they is "everyone", which is singular.
2. a) his
   b) Decay commonly attacks our teeth, and they are eventually painful.
   c) which
   d) he or she

Adverb Errors (page 76)

Here are some words you might have used.

1. very or exceptionally (adverbs to modify the adjective, sweet)
2. slow or old (adjectives to modify the noun, process)
3. very (adverb to modify the adjective, special)
4. wisely or regularly (adverbs to modify the verb, followed) good or fine (adjectives to modify the noun, example)

Conjunctions (page 77)

1. Whether; or
2. neither; nor
3. either; or
4. both; and

Double Negatives (page 78)

1. We have never found out the actual date of the first Olympic games, but tradition places the date at 776 B.C.
2. The Greeks hardly ever (or never) forgot that Zeus was the god in whose honour the games were held.
3. Today, however, one barely remembers that the Olympics began as a religious festival.

Redundancy and Repetition (page 79)

Here are some ways the sentences can be revised.

1. The famous Canadian author, Stephen Leacock, once discussed whether the bicycle or the horse is the nobler creature.
2. Leacock points out that the horse is covered with hair.
3. The bicycle, though, is not covered with hair, except for the 1889 model that is ridden in Idaho.
4. He concludes that he now understands why horsemen spend so little time sitting when they are not on their horses.

Mixed Metaphors (page 80)

Here are some ways you can revise the sentences:

1. Don has been losing weight quickly.
2. I sat down to type a letter to the employment office.
3. As we embark on the road of life, we should remember that our goals are the best maps.

Tone and Sentence Type (page 80)

1. statement or exclamation (. or !) depending on tone of voice.
2. command (.)
3. question (?)
4. statement or exclamation (.) or (!) depending on tone of voice.

Word Order and Ideas (page 81)

The emphasis in each of the three sentences can be changed by moving the underlined words to the front of the sentence.

1. Critically important in a disaster is the availability of heat, light, shelter, food, and water.
2. Because regular medical personnel are rarely able to keep up with the increased demand for services, people who know first aid are indispensable in any kind of disaster.
3. Food and water are considered by most of us to be the primary necessities of life; however, one winter night spent in the open air without heat or light would probably cause us to reorder our priorities.

Spelling (page 86)

Sentence 1 dramatically, course

Sentence 2 desirable, transportation, freight, running, their

Sentence 3 choose, usually, receive, personnel, denies, slowly, to

Sentence 4 believe, noticeable, airfares

Sentence 5 truly, skies, preferred

Hyphenated Words (page 88)

Sentence 1 ten-year-old, city-wide

Sentence 2 hundred-metre

Sentence 3 eight-fifteen, great-grandmother

Sentence 4 self-conscious

Regular and Irregular Words (page 92)

Here are the sentences with the correct forms. The underlined words are the ones that were incorrect.

Today, all children should learn to cook. In many families, both husbands and wives share in meal preparation. Gone are the days when men could get away with knowing how to make only a few dishes.

2. Too, people are using less frozen food. Basic ingredients like potatoes and tomatoes have found their way back into our diets.
3. Of ccurse, foods that have already been prepared by manufacturers are often easier to prepare, but they are not necessarily better than homemade foods. Mostly, they are selected because they are sure to reach the table sooner than homemade foods.
4. When TV dinners first hit the market, they were swept off the supermarket shelves by eager buyers. But gradually, people found that these items were more expensive than the same meals made from scratch.

Usage (page 95)

The underlined words were incorrect.

1. All except a few of the world's zoos are more humane today than they were in past years.
2. Specially trained people are available to advise zoo personnel, whose job it is to care for the animals.
3. In most facilities, it's possible for the animals to run loose in quite large areas whenever they choose.
4. Of course, you're likely to see the odd animal in a cage, but changes are it's there for observation on the orders of a veterinarian.

Word Division (page 97)

1. easy- / going
2. too short to divide
3. quan- / tity
4. proper name, no division
5. too short to divide
6. sour- / dough

Abbreviations (page 98)

The underlined words and phrases were incorrect.

1. On <u>Sunday</u>, <u>7 December 1941</u>, the Japanese bombed Pearl Harbour.
2. <u>United States President</u> Roosevelt immediately declared war on Japan.
3. Canada was already at war with the Germans, but the attack made <u>Christmas</u> even sadder that year.
4. From St. John to Vancouver, Canadians experienced hardships in <u>World War II</u>; rationing, the draft, bad news, <u>and so on</u> made life difficult.

Numbers (page 100)

1. fifty; ten
2. 145; forty-five, thirty-five
3. five

Capital Letters (page 102)

Here are the sentences with the correct forms.

1. Surely my uncle didn't intend to fight the battle of the Plains of Abraham again!
2. "We're going to meet General Montcalm and his forces," said Uncle François, "and this time we'll win the battle."
3. The Seven Years' War would never have ended as it did if my crazy uncle had been fighting.
4. As he often says, someone could then have written a book called The Five Days' War.

Punctuation (page 111)

1. The correct punctuation has been added and circled.

What would you say is the twentieth century's greatest contribution to literature? If you're like most people, after a moment's thought, you'll probably say, "Science fiction." Surprisingly, this common answer is not precisely correct; it's only half right. The reason why this answer is only half right is simple: Two of the greatest science fiction writers of all time did most of their best writing before the year 1900. They are Jules Verne and H.G. Wells. Verne's famous *Twenty Thousand Leagues Under the Sea* was published in 1870; Wells' classic *The Time Machine* first appeared in 1895, and his terrifying *The War of the Worlds* came out in 1898.

2. Here are the corrected grammar tips.

   Verbs have to agree with their subjects.

   Never use double negatives.

   Avoid unnecessary commas.

   Don't use run-on sentences; they are hard to read.

   Use all adverbs correctly.

   Everyone should be careful to use a singular pronoun with singular nouns in his or her writing.

   Dangling modifiers must be avoided.

   Check carefully to see if you left any words out.

   Spell correctly.

   Think carefully about sentence fragments.

   Repeating a word is not usually effective.

   Avoid mixed metaphors.

   Avoid clichés.

CHAPTER 6: LETTERS

Letters (page 136)

Here is a list of the errors and omissions.

1. There is no return address.
2. There is no postal code for the recipient.
3. A salutation in a Business Letter uses a colon, not a comma.
4. The writer doesn't state when in July— the whole month? first week?
5. How many in the group? This may affect the rate.
6. There is no stamped, self-addressed envelope enclosed for a reply.
7. "Thank you" is not an appropriate closing; use "Sincerely".
8. The closing is punctuated with a comma, not a colon.
9. The writer did not type his or her name under the signature. The signature is illegible. With no return address and an illegible name, the writer cannot hope to receive a reply.

CHAPTER 7: LISTENING AND SPEAKING

Listening and Speaking (page 153)

1. something hard to write on
2. use the cards as reminders only; write one note on each card; write phrases instead of sentences; write big so you can see the note at a glance
3. the title and purpose of your project.
4. volume of your voice; your pace; your eye contact; how you stand; your tone of voice; your effectiveness with note cards; how natural you seem
5. arrive on time; prepare a list of questions in advance; organize the questions in order of importance; do not spend too much time on any one question; watch the time you are using carefully

Index